本教材获教育部中外语言交流合作中心项目资助项目号 21YH052CX5

Basic Legal Chinese

马琳琳 — 编著

基础法律汉语（上册）

中国政法大学出版社
2025·北京

图书在版编目（CIP）数据

基础法律汉语. 上册 / 马琳琳编著. -- 北京 ：中
国政法大学出版社，2025. 1. -- ISBN 978-7-5764-1895-8

Ⅰ. H195.4

中国国家版本馆 CIP 数据核字第 2025A5R719 号

书　　名	基础法律汉语（上册）JI CHU FA LÜ HAN YU （ SHANG CE ）	
出 版 者	中国政法大学出版社	
地　　址	北京市海淀区西土城路25号	
邮　　箱	fadapress@163.com	
网　　址	http://www.cuplpress.com (网络实名：中国政法大学出版社)	
电　　话	010-58908435(第一编辑部) 58908334(邮购部)	
承　　印	北京中科印刷有限公司	
开　　本	720mm×960mm　　1/16	
印　　张	13.75	
字　　数	203千字	
版　　次	2025年1月第1版	
印　　次	2025年1月第1次印刷	
定　　价	69.00元	

作者简介

　　马琳琳，河南郑州人。博士。中国政法大学国际教育学院教师。师从中央民族大学张公瑾先生修读语言学及应用语言学、师从中国政法大学朱勇教授修读中国法律史。学术研究领域包括：语言学及应用语言学、中国法律史、国际中文教育等。

前　言

　　中国法律文明源远流长。从先秦时期到今天，始终在不断进步。而伴随中国历史的发展脉络，中国古代法律传统和法律文化逐渐形成并演进，与中华法系共融共生，不仅是中国历史的一部分，更是中华文明的一部分。

　　中国古代法律文化的核心是"礼法"，并自汉代开始，逐渐与儒家思想相融合。随着历史阶段的演变，各个朝代在法律建设上既有继承又有创新，形成了丰富的具有中国特色的法律传统。

适用对象

　　本教材适用于具有中文中级以上水平的国际学生，也可以作为中文以及中国文化学习者的参考资料。

编写理念

　　本教材以中国法律史和法律文化发展的脉络为主线，可使学习者在中国古代法律的发展历程与法文化中学习中文。因此，教材不仅仅关注中国法律史与法律文化本身，更从中文学习的角度出发，帮助学习者了解中文深层的文化底色。

编写原则

　　本教材在编写过程中，力求做到以下几点：首先，注重中国法律发展史的脉络；其次，强调法律发展过程中与社会文化的互动；最后，通过法文化展现中文的语言特色。

教材结构

本教材分为上下两册，每册 12 课，共 24 课。其中，上册从中国法律的起源到唐朝；下册从宋朝到清朝末年。每课教学课时建议为 3—4 课时。本册为教材的上册。每课主要安排如下：

【课前准备】与本课相关的中国历史发展简介

【导　　读】与本课课文相关的中国法律史内容

【课　　文】需要重点了解的中国法律史、法文化相关内容，及相关生词

【重点汉字】本课重点学习的法文化高频字

【文化知识】与本课所涉历史朝代相关的中国历史文化知识

【法治文物】与中国法文化相关的法治文物

【经典阅读】与本课所涉历史朝代相关的古代典籍

主要特色

本教材最大的特色是：以中国法律制度史为纲，以系统性的法律文化知识为桥梁，进行中文学习，特别在每一课列出中国法文化的高频字。其中，高频字的选取以《说文解字》为基础、以《唐律疏议》为参考、根据法律词语语域界定的标准，并结合现代法学概念和出现的频率。教材同时配有沉浸式动画版，学习者可以扫描下页二维码进入学习。

特别致谢

中国政法大学法律史学研究院 朱勇教授

中国政法大学法律古籍整理研究所 李雪梅教授

我们希望，通过本教材，学习者能够在掌握中国古代法律基本知识的基础上，形成对中国法律文化的全面认识，并对中文有更深入的了解；进而为理解和参与现代法治建设提供历史借鉴和文化滋养。

编　者

2024 年 8 月

本教材所用语法术语及缩略语形式参照表

Grammar Terms in Chinese	Grammar Terms in English	Abbreviations
名词	noun	*n.*
动词	verb	*v.*
形容词	adjective	*adj.*
介词	preposition	*prep.*
成语	idiom	*idm.*
短语	phrase	*phr.*
专有名词	proper noun	*proper n.*

本教材沉浸式动画下载地址

目 录

CONTENTS

第一课

华夏文明与中国法律的起源

课 前准备

图 1-1 陕西神木石峁遗址：黄帝部落都邑

法律与国家、民族、社会，密不可分。因此，中国法律史与中国历史在发展上，是沿着同一条历史道路行进，集中体现了中华民族在经济、政治、社会等各方面的进步。

中国古代法制的一大特点是引礼入法。作为汉语一级字的"礼"，最早见于甲骨文，是一个会意字。从示、从豊，"豊"是行礼之器，下部为"豆"，字本义为盛食物的器皿。所以"礼"字本义是击鼓献玉、供奉神灵，举行仪典，祭神求福。

Law is inseparable from the state, the nation, and society. Therefore, the history of Chinese law and the broader history of China have developed along the same historical path, reflecting the progress of the Chinese nation in economics, politics, and society.

A distinctive feature of ancient Chinese legal systems was the incorporation of ritual into law. The first-level Chinese character "礼", meaning ritual, is a compound ideogram that first appeared in oracle bone inscriptions. It is composed of the elements "示" and "豊", where "豊" represents a ritual vessel and the lower part "豆" signifies a container. The original meaning of the character refers to a vessel used for holding food. Thus, the original meaning of "礼" involved beating drums to present jade offerings and worship spirits, it was used in ceremonies to worship gods and seek blessings.

 生词表

序号	生词	词性	汉语拼音	英文解释
1	法律史	*n.*	fǎ lǜ shǐ	legal history
2	引礼入法	*phr.*	yǐn lǐ rù fǎ	integrate rites into laws
3	一级字	*n.*	yī jí zì	first-level character（in complexity）
4	甲骨文	*n.*	jiǎ gǔ wén	oracle bone script
5	会意字	*n.*	huì yì zì	ideogram
6	行礼之器	*n.*	xíng lǐ zhī qì	ritual vessel
7	豆	*n.*	dòu	vessel（in ancient contexts）
8	供奉	*v.*	gòng fèng	offer sacrifices to the gods
9	仪典	*n.*	yí diǎn	ceremony
10	祭神求福	*phr.*	jì shén qiú fú	worship gods and seek blessings

 读

中国法律的产生经历了一个漫长的演进过程。新石器时代后期，三大部落联盟出于对外扩张以及在相互征战中维系自身存在与发展的需要，更加注重内部秩序的建立和维持。部落联盟在职能机构的设置以及对不同类型社会关系的调整等方面，已形成大量处理争端的判决以及确定某些事项的决定，并进而形成性质各异、功能不同的规范体系。其中相当一部分已为社会所承认和接受，具有普遍适用性和一定程度的强制性，从而已初步具备法律的特征。[1]

课 文

　　在古代中国的部落联盟时期，各部落之间形成了一种复杂的社会和政治关系。其中，黄帝部落是一个非常重要的部落，他们建立了一套官职体系来管理内部事务。根据《史记·五帝本纪》的记载，黄帝设置了许多官职，如"云师"等，用以组织和管理他的军队。除此之外，还设有监察官来监督其他部落，确保他们的忠诚和服从。

　　黄帝统治时，他要求其他部落定期向他交纳财物。如果不服从，黄帝就会发动战争。这种做法在《史记·五帝本纪》中有所记载：**"轩辕乃习用干戈，以征不享"**。这说明黄帝用武力来确保他的权威。

　　在这个时期，大禹是另一位重要的领袖。他接受了上一代领袖帝舜的命令，继承了他的职责，开始进行大规模的水利工程，以治理频繁的洪水灾害。经过大约十年的努力，禹成功地通过疏导河流的方式控制了洪水。但帝舜让禹治理水患的目的不仅仅是防洪，更重要的是"平土"，即巡视各地，对已经臣服的部落进行地理上的划分，分为"九州"。根据土地的肥沃程度和部落对帝舜的服从程度，禹还制定了不同级别的税收标准。为了保证帝舜的命令能够顺利传达到这些部落，并加强中央与地方的联系，确保税赋的顺利收取，禹还改善了通往这些部落的道路。

　　在部落联盟时期，南方的苗族和中原的黄帝部落分别有着不同的刑罚制度。根据《尚书·吕刑》的记载，南方苗族的刑罚非常残酷，包括割鼻、割耳、破坏生殖功能和在脸上刺字等。这反映了他们独特的生活习俗和社会结构。而在中原黄帝部落，也形成了一套强制性行为规范的刑罚体系。《商君书·画策》中提到，在神农时代，人们的生活比较简单和平和，不需要严格的

---

〔1〕　参见朱勇主编：《中国法律史》，中国政法大学出版社 2021 版，第 3~4 页。

刑法。但在神农去世后，随着社会的发展，出现了强者欺凌弱者、多数暴力少数的情况，因此黄帝开始制定各种法律和规范，包括家庭和社会的伦理规范，以及使用武力和刑罚来维护社会秩序。这些刑罚多是对身体的直接伤害，如用刀、锯等工具对犯罪者进行肢体刑罚，以此来惩罚和威慑不遵守规则的人。

图 1-2　中国考古博物馆：玉猪龙 新石器时代红山文化

在帝尧时期，这种基于身体惩罚的刑罚仍然被使用。帝尧是一位伟大的领袖，他沿用了这种刑罚方式，继续维护社会的秩序和稳定。

 原文参考

《史记·五帝本纪》载，黄帝"以师兵为营卫，官名皆以云命，为云师。置左右大监，监于万国……举风后、力牧、常先、大鸿以治民"。

《史记·五帝本纪》："于是轩辕乃习用干戈，以征不享。"

《尚书·吕刑》载："苗民弗用灵，制以刑，惟作五虐之刑曰法。杀戮无辜，爰始淫为劓、刵、椓、黥，越兹丽刑并制，罔差有辞。"

《商君书·画策》："神农之世，男耕而食，妇织而衣，刑政不用而治，甲兵不起而王。神农既没，以强胜弱，以众暴寡，故黄帝作为君臣上下之义，父子兄弟之礼，夫妇妃匹之合，内行刀锯，外用甲兵。"

生词表

序号	生词	词性	汉语拼音	英文解释
1	部落联盟	n.	bù luò lián méng	tribal alliance
2	复杂	adj.	fù zá	complex
3	官职体系	phr.	guān zhí tǐ xì	official system
4	内部事务	phr.	nèi bù shì wù	internal affairs
5	云师	proper n.	Yún shī	title of an official
6	监察官	n.	jiān chá guān	inspector
7	轩辕	proper n.	Xuān yuán	name of Yellow Emperor
8	干戈	n.	gān gē	arms, warfare
9	征	v.	zhēng	conquer, campaign
10	不享	phr.	bù xiǎng	not to submit
11	水利工程	n.	shuǐ lì gōng chéng	hydraulic engineering
12	洪水灾害	n.	hóng shuǐ zāi hài	flood disaster
13	疏导	v.	shū dǎo	dredge, divert
14	平土	n.	píng tǔ	leveling land
15	巡视	v.	xún shì	inspect
16	九州	proper n.	Jiǔ zhōu	Nine Provinces of ancient China
17	税收标准	phr.	shuì shōu biāo zhǔn	tax standards
18	刑罚制度	phr.	xíng fá zhì dù	penal system
19	割鼻	phr.	gē bí	cut off the nose
20	割耳	phr.	gē ěr	cut off the ears
21	刺字	phr.	cì zì	tattoo the face
22	强制性	adj.	qiáng zhì xìng	compulsory
23	画策	n.	huà cè	strategy, policy
24	神农	proper n.	Shén nóng	name of a legendary ruler

重 点汉字【"灋"（法）】

法，金文写作"灋"，最早见于西周，由"氵（水）""廌（zhì）""去"三部分组成。"廌"为獬豸，是古代传说中一种掌司法断案的神兽，能明辨善恶是非，杨孚《异物志》记载："东北荒中有兽，名獬豸，一角，性忠，见人斗，则触不直者。"因此，法是一个会意字，意思是"衡平若水，去伪存真"，这是中国古代神权法思想在语言文字上的体现。

图 1-3 "法"字篆刻（王琦 刻）

 汉字拓展

序号	词汇	汉语拼音	英文解释	例句
1	法律	fǎ lǜ	law	这项新法律旨在提高道路安全性。
2	法规	fǎ guī	regulations	公司必须遵守所有相关的环境保护法规。
3	法院	fǎ yuàn	court	他因交通违规被传唤至法院。
4	法宝	fǎ bǎo	magical treasure	古代传说中，这位仙人拥有一件神奇的法宝。
5	法师	fǎ shī	mage，wizard	在这个游戏里，我选择扮演一名法师。

续表

序号	词汇	汉语拼音	英文解释	例句
6	法语	fǎ yǔ	French language	她在大学主修法语。
7	法国	Fǎ guó	France	我们计划明年夏天去法国旅行。
8	程序法	chéng xù fǎ	procedural law	程序法确保了司法过程的公正性。
9	刑法	xíng fǎ	criminal law	刑法规定了对犯罪行为的惩罚。
10	民法	mín fǎ	civil law	民法调整个人与个人之间的私法关系。
11	法学	fǎ xué	jurisprudence	他在法学院学习，准备成为一名律师。
12	法轮	fǎ lún	Dharma wheel	法轮在佛教中象征着教法的传播。

文 化知识【獬豸】

图 1-4　陕西历史博物馆：北朝·独角兽

獬豸（xiè zhì），在中国古代神话和传说中，是一种象征正义和诚实的神兽，通常被描述为一种类似独角兽的神兽，具有独角和类似狮子或其他猛兽的身体。它的独角象征着辨别是非的能力。

在神话传说中，獬豸被认为能够准确地辨别罪恶和无辜，因此成为正义和公正的象征。它的形象常被用于法院和审判场所，古代法律文书、印章以及其他与法律相关的物品上，以象征公正无私的审判。

在中国古代的文学作品中，獬豸经常被提及，作为道德和正义的代表。獬豸的象征意义在于其超凡的判断力和公正无私的特质，它代表了理想的司法精神和公正无私的审判，它不仅体现了古代中国人对法律和正义的追求，也反映了中国传统文化中关于道德和法治的理念。

法 治文物【"獬豸"博物馆（一）】

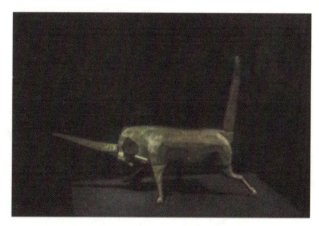

图 1-5 西汉·木雕独角兽[1]

经 典阅读

《列仙传·黄帝》[2]：黄帝者，号曰轩辕。能劾百神，朝而使之。弱而能言，圣而预知，知物之纪。自以为云师，有龙形。自择亡日，与群臣辞。至于卒，还葬桥山，山崩，柩空无尸，唯剑舄在焉。《仙书》云：黄帝采首山之铜，铸鼎于荆山之下，鼎成，有龙垂胡髯下迎帝，乃升天。群臣百僚悉持龙髯，从帝而升，攀帝弓及龙髯，拔而弓坠，群臣不得从，望帝而悲号。故后

---

〔1〕 参见李雪梅：《谜一样的独角兽（一）》，载《中国法律评论》2021 年第 2 期。
〔2〕 选自林屋译注：《列仙传》，中华书局 2021 年版，第 15 页。

世以其处为鼎湖，名其弓为乌号焉。

神圣渊玄，邈哉帝皇。暂莅万物，冠名百王。化周六合，数通无方。假葬桥山，超升昊苍。

 ## 参考译文

黄帝，也被称为轩辕。他能召集并驱使百神，年幼时就能用语言清晰地表达自己的思想，圣智超群，能够预知未来，了解万物的规律。他自称为云师，具有龙的形态。他自己选择了逝世的日期，并与群臣告别。到了他去世的时候，安葬于桥山，但山崩塌后，棺木空空如也，没有尸体，只留下剑和鞋。《仙书》中说：黄帝在首山采铜，于荆山之下铸造了鼎。铸鼎完成之时，有龙降临，胡须垂下迎接黄帝，于是他便升天了。群臣和百官都抓住龙的胡须想跟从黄帝一同升天，他们攀附于黄帝的弓和龙的胡须，但龙须脱落、弓也突然坠落，群臣未能随黄帝一同上升，只能望着黄帝升天而悲痛呼号。因此，后世将这个地方称为鼎湖，那把弓被命名为乌号。

黄帝的神性深奥莫测，多么高远啊，帝皇。他短暂地出现在世间，超越了百王之上。他的变化覆盖天下，他的命运通达变化无穷。他假身托葬于桥山，然后超凡升入广阔的天空。

The Yellow Emperor, also known as Xuanyuan, could summon and command hundreds of deities. Despite his youth, he was eloquent, divinely wise, and capable of foreseeing the future, understanding the laws of all things. He claimed to be Yunshi: bearing the form of a dragon. He chose his own day of death and bid farewell to his ministers. Upon his death, he was buried in Qiao Mountain, but when the mountain collapsed, the coffin was found empty without a corpse, leaving only a sword and shoes behind. According to *Xian Shu*: The Yellow Emperor gathered copper from Shou Mountain and cast a cauldron under Jing Mountain. When the cauldron was completed, a dragon descended, its whiskers hanging down to welcome the Yellow Emperor, and thus he ascended to heaven. All the ministers and officials clutched the dragon's whiskers to ascend with the emperor. They clung to the emperor's bow and the dragon's whiskers, but when the dragon's whiskers and bow suddenly fell, the ministers could not ascend with the emperor and could only watch him ascend to heaven while they cried out in grief. Therefore, later generations called this place Ding Lake, and the bow was named Wuhao.

The Yellow Emperor's divinity was profound and inscrutable. How lofty is the Emperoer! He appeared briefly in the world, surpassing a hundred kings. His transformation encompassed the six directions, and his knowledge of numbers was boundless. He feigned burial in Qiao Mountain, then transcended and ascended into the vast sky.

课 后练习

1. 选择题：根据《史记·五帝本纪》，黄帝设置的"云师"官职的主要职责是什么？

A. 组织和管理军队

B. 监督财务

C. 收集和记录文献

D. 监察其他部落

2. 判断题：黄帝通过战争来确保其他部落的服从。

3. 填空题：大禹治理洪水的主要方法是 _____。

4. 简答题：描述南方苗族与黄帝部落在刑罚制度上的主要区别。

5. 讨论题：帝尧时期基于身体惩罚的刑法如何维护社会秩序和稳定。提供具体的历史背景和刑罚实例以支持你的观点。

课 文参考翻译

During the period of tribal alliances in ancient China, a complex social and political relationship developed among the tribes. Among these, the Yellow Emperor's tribe was particularly important, establishing a system of official positions to manage internal affairs. According to *The Records of the Grand Historian: Five Emperors' Annals*, the Yellow Emperor established numerous official positions, such as the "Cloud Master," to organize and manage his army. Additionally, supervisory officials were appointed to oversee other tribes, ensuring their loyalty and obedience.

Under the Yellow Emperor's rule, he required other tribes to regularly tribute goods to him. If they did not comply, the Yellow Emperor would wage war against them. This practice is documented in *The Records of The Grand Historian: Five Emperors' Annals:* "Xuanyuan thus practiced using weapons to conquer those who did not submit," indicating that the Yellow Emperor used force to assert his authority.

During this period, Yu the Great was another significant leader. He received orders from the previous leader, Emperor Shun, and inherited his duties, initiating large-scale hydraulic projects to control the frequent flooding. After approximately ten years of effort, Yu successfully controlled the floods by diverting rivers. However, Emperor Shun's intention for Yu to manage the floods was not only for flood control but also for "leveling the land," meaning to survey the territories and geographically divide the already submissive tribes into "Nine Provinces." Based on the fertility of the land and the degree of loyalty to Emperor Shun, Yu also established different levels of tax standards. To ensure that Emperor Shun's orders could be smoothly communicated to these tribes and to strengthen the connection between the central and local areas, especially to ensure the smooth collection of taxes, Yu improved the roads leading to these tribes.

During the period of tribal alliances, the southern Miao tribe and the Yellow Emperor tribe in the central plains had different penal systems. According to *The Book of Documents: Lü Xing*, the southern Miao tribe had extremely harsh punishments, including cutting off the nose, cutting off the ears, mutilating reproductive organs, and tattooing the face. This reflected their unique customs and social structure. In the Yellow Emperor tribe in the central plains, a penal system based on compulsory behavioral norms had formed. *The Book of Lord Shang : Strategies* mentions that during the time of the Shen Nong, people's lives were relatively simple and peaceful, not requiring strict laws. However, after the Shen Nong's death, with the development of society, instances of the strong bullying the weak and majority violence against minorities emerged, prompting the Yellow Emperor to formulate various laws and norms, including family and social ethics, and the use of force and punishment to maintain social order. These punishments often involved direct bodily harm, such as using knives and saws for corporal punishment, to punish and deter those who did not follow the rules.

In the time of Emperor Yao, this form of corporal punishment-based penal system was still in use. Emperor Yao, a great leader, continued this punitive method to maintain social order and stability.

夏商时期的法律

前准备

图 2-1　中国考古博物馆：镶嵌绿松石兽面纹铜牌饰 河南偃师二里头文化

根据史书记载，在公元前 21 世纪，夏启建立夏王朝，被视为中国历史上第一个王朝，即所谓"夏传子，家天下"。据载，夏朝存在四百余年，在夏桀统治时期被商所灭。商汤在公元前 16 世纪建立商朝，商朝后来迁都至殷（今安阳），因此商朝又被称为"殷"或"殷商"。商朝存在约六百年，在商纣王统治时期被周所灭。夏商时期属于中国古代法律发展的早期，夏商法律也体现出古代文明早期法律的基本特征。由于文献记载和出土资料的匮乏，我们对夏朝法律及相关内容所知不多，只能从零散的文献资料中略知一二。商灭夏建立统治之后，在夏朝法律的基础上进一步发展自己的法律及相关制度。[1]

According to historical records, in the 21st century BC, Qi established the Xia Dynasty, regarded as the first dynasty in Chinese history, commonly referred to as "Xia passing the rule to his descendants, governing all under heaven." It is recorded that the Xia Dynasty lasted for over four hundred

---

〔1〕 参见朱勇主编：《中国法律史》，中国政法大学出版社 2021 年版，第 16 页。

years and was overthrown during the reign of Jie, the last Xia ruler, by the Shang. In the 16th century BC, Tang of Shang established the Shang Dynasty, which later moved its capital to Yin（present-day Anyang）, hence the dynasty is also referred to as "Yin" or "Yin Shang." The Shang Dynasty lasted about six hundred years and was destroyed by the Zhou during the reign of King Zhou, the last Shang ruler. The Xia and Shang periods represent the early stages of legal development in ancient China, reflecting the basic characteristics of early civilization's laws. Due to the scarcity of documentary records and archaeological findings, our knowledge of the Xia Dynasty's laws and related content is limited, gleaned only from sparse documentary sources. After the Shang overthrew the Xia, they further developed their own legal and related systems based on the legal foundations of the Xia.

 生词表

序号	生词	词性	汉语拼音	英文解释
1	夏启	*proper n.*	Xià Qǐ	King Qi of Xia
2	王朝	*n.*	wáng cháo	dynasty
3	夏桀	*proper n.*	Xià Jié	King Jie of Xia
4	商汤	*proper n.*	Shāng Tāng	King Tang of Shang
5	殷	*proper n.*	Yīn	another name for Shang dynasty
6	商纣王	*proper n.*	Shāng zhòu wáng	King Zhou of Shang
7	文献	*n.*	wén xiàn	documents, archives
8	出土	*v.*	chū tǔ	unearth, excavate
9	资料	*n.*	zī liào	materials, data
10	匮乏	*adj.*	kuì fá	scarce, insufficient
11	零散	*adj.*	líng sǎn	fragmented, scattered
12	建立	*v.*	jiàn lì	establish, set up

基础法律汉语（上册）

导 读

在远古时期，人们的生存环境较为恶劣，对自然界的事物和自然现象的认识有限，存在着很多当时人不能理解和解释的事物，对于风雨雷电等现象也多有敬畏。泛灵论在早期的诸多民族中存在，认为万物有灵。这些崇敬神灵的现象及其产生的宗教观念是当时人类生活和社会环境的产物。据载，夏商时期存在浓厚的图腾崇拜和祖先崇拜，并在政治统治和国家治理方面产生了神权法思想，将神灵（上天）视为统治的基础和合法性来源。[1]

课 文

夏商统治者宣称自己是受上天的委托、秉承上天的旨意进行统治的，即"受命于天"。《尚书·召诰》记载：**"有夏服天命"，"有殷受天命"**。对于商朝的产生，《诗经·商颂·玄鸟》写到：**"天命玄鸟，降而生商"**。这一方面彰显了统治的神圣性，另一方面也彰显了统治的权威性和合法性，即"受天命"而行统治之权。也因此，统治者发布的命令、颁布的法律都是"神意"的体现，不容置喙。

在商朝的文献记载及出土的甲骨文中，经常可以看到商朝人尊崇上天的内容（如图 2-2 的甲骨卜辞）。根据学界考证，此为存世最大的完整刻辞肩胛骨。内容为前后十余日贞问，用羊等祭牲向殷先公和岳神施行燎祭，询问哪天会下雨。

甲骨文中类似的记载有很多。由此可见商朝人对于上天的崇拜。商朝统治者将政治统治与对祖先的崇拜和对上天的崇拜联系在一起，也说明统治者的统治权力来源于"上天"或祖先的安排，是根据上天或祖先的意旨而进行的。

---

〔1〕参见朱勇主编：《中国法律史》，中国政法大学出版社 2021 年版，第 16 页。

除了"受命于天"的思想之外，夏商的统治者还"恭行天罚"，把自己对其他部族或者反对势力的征伐或惩戒，宣称为根据上天的旨意而进行的惩罚。例如，夏启在征伐有扈氏时就声称是"恭行天之罚"：**"天用剿绝其命，今予惟恭行天之罚"**（《尚书·甘誓》）。商汤灭夏时也是打着"上帝"的旗号进行的，《尚书·汤誓》记载：**"有夏多罪，天命殛之"**，商汤还说，因**"夏氏有罪"**，**"予畏上帝，不敢不正"**。因其敬畏"上帝"，征伐夏是"上帝"的旨意，所以商汤灭夏是"恭行天罚"，不敢不去征伐。

图 2-2　国家典籍博物馆：商朝·刻辞甲骨[1]

　　夏商的统治者通过"神判"、依据卜辞而施行法令的做法，既可以让民众敬畏信服，也有利于维护统治阶层的统治和稳定。[2]

―――――――――――――

　　〔1〕　参见国家典籍博物馆甲骨注释："北图 5405　商武乙文丁时期（前 1147—前 1102）历组 兽骨 43.5×24 厘米面 196 字、背 22 字 刘体智旧藏《甲骨文合集》33747 著录。"卜辞释文："面：……三（10）丙子卜，丁雨。（11）丙子卜，戊雨。三（12）丙子卜，燎（），雨。三（13）丙子卜，（）、雨。三（14）丙子卜，（）弗雨。（15）丙子卜，（）雨。三（16）戊寅，雨。三（17）戊寅卜，已允雨。三（18）庚晨卜，雨。三（19）庚辰卜，辛雨。一（20）庚晨卜，壬雨。一（21）甲申卜，（）目岳羊。三（22）甲申卜，（）十火。一（23）甲申卜，（）十火。二（24）甲申卜，（）十火。三（25）甲申卜，丙雨。二（26）甲申卜，丁雨。（27）乙酉卜，丙戌雨……背：（1）丁丑卜。（2）戊辰，雨。（3）戊辰，不雨。（4）二日，今雨已已。（5）癸亥力乞肩三。"

　　〔2〕　参见朱勇主编：《中国法律史》，中国政法大学出版社 2021 年版，第 16~21 页。

 生词表

序号	生词	词性	汉语拼音	英文解释
1	宣称	*v.*	xuān chēng	proclaim，declare
2	秉承	*v.*	bǐng chéng	uphold，inherit
3	旨意	*n.*	zhǐ yì	will，intention
4	神圣性	*n.*	shén shèng xìng	sanctity
5	权威性	*n.*	quán wēi xìng	authoritativeness
6	合法性	*n.*	hé fǎ xìng	legitimacy
7	置喙	*v.*	zhì huì	meddle，interfere
8	尊崇	*v.*	zūn chóng	revere，esteem
9	肩胛骨	*n.*	jiān jiǎ gǔ	scapula，shoulder blade
10	贞问	*n.*	zhēn wèn	divination inquiry
11	燎祭	*n.*	liáo jì	burning sacrifice
12	族群	*n.*	zú qún	ethnic group，tribe
13	征伐	*v.*	zhēng fá	campaign against，attack
14	惩戒	*n.*	chéng jiè	punishment，disciplinary action
15	汤誓	*proper n.*	Tāng shì	Oath of King Tang
16	夏氏	*proper n.*	Xià shì	the Xia clan
17	神判	*n.*	shén pàn	divine judgement
18	依据	*prep.*	yī jù	according to
19	卜辞	*n.*	bǔ cí	divination text
20	施行	*v.*	shī xíng	implement，carry out
21	敬畏	*v.*	jìng wèi	revere，awe
22	统治阶层	*phr.*	tǒng zhì jiē céng	ruling class

重 点汉字【律】

　　律，原本是中国古代审定乐音高低的标准。古时把声音分为六律（阳律）和六品（阴律），合称"十二律"。《千字文》中写道"律吕调阳"，其中，"律吕"指古代用竹管制成的校正乐律的器具，以管的长短来确定音的不同高度，从低音管算起，成奇数的六个管称"律"，成偶数的六个管称"吕"，后来"律吕"成为音律的统称。根据《康熙字典》的释义，《说文》中将"律"解释为"均布也"；《尔雅·释诂》引申为"法也"；《周易·师卦》中把军法称为"律"，"师出以律"；《晋书·刑法志》中，将刑书称为"律"："承用秦汉旧律，其文起自魏文师侯李悝"。

图 2-3　"律"字篆刻 （王琦 刻）

 汉字拓展

序号	词汇	汉语拼音	英文解释	例句
1	律师	lǜ shī	lawyer	律师正在法庭上辩护。
2	律法	lǜ fǎ	statutes，laws	古代的律法比现在的要严格得多。
3	乐律	yuè lǜ	musical rhythm	这首曲子的乐律很独特。
4	节律	jié lǜ	rhythm	这首诗的节律非常和谐。
5	律动	lǜ dòng	rhythmical movement	孩子们在音乐的律动下欢快地跳舞。

续表

序号	词汇	汉语拼音	英文解释	例句
6	自律	zì lǜ	self-discipline	他非常自律，每天早上都会去跑步。
7	韵律	yùn lǜ	prosody，rhyme	这首诗的韵律优美，令人印象深刻。
8	声律	shēng lǜ	sound law，phonology	语言学家在研究不同语言之间的声律关系。

化知识【皋陶】

图2-4　汉魏·《皋陶治狱图》画像石[1]

　　皋陶（Gāo yáo）是中国上古时期的一位重要神话人物，他在中国神话和古代文献中被赋予了许多重要的角色和职责。其中，皋陶最著名的身份是中国古代法律制度的奠基人之一。据传，他是第一个制定刑法的人，尤其是

　　〔1〕 参见《汉魏·〈皋陶治狱图〉画像石》，载中国政法大学中华法制文明虚拟博物馆，https://flgj.cupl.edu.cn/info/1092/2778.htm，最后访问日期：2024年10月22日。

在尧、舜两代时期。他的法律思想强调公正和适用性，他的刑法被称为"皋陶刑"。

　　皋陶不仅在法律方面有贡献，他还是一位道德模范。在古代文献中，他经常被描述为正直、公正的理想官员，是后代官吏的楷模。此外，他通常被描绘成具有智慧和远见的人物，能够预见并解决复杂的社会问题。皋陶的故事在《尚书》《史记》等多部古代文献中有所记载，虽然这些记载中的细节有所不同，但都强调了他在法律和治国方面的贡献。

　　总的来说，皋陶在中国文化中是法律、正义和道德的象征，被后世尊崇为法治和公正的典范。他的故事和形象在中国的历史和文化中占有重要地位。

法　治文物【"獬豸"博物馆（二）】

图 2-5　汉·彩绘木雕独角兽[1]

经　典阅读

　　《列仙传·彭祖》[2]：彭祖者，殷大夫也。姓籛名铿，帝颛顼之孙陆终氏之

---

　　〔1〕　参见李雪梅：《谜一样的独角兽（一）》，载《中国法律评论》2021 年第 2 期。

　　〔2〕　选自林屋译注：《列仙传》，中华书局 2021 年版，第 60 页。

中子，历夏至殷末八百馀岁。常食佳芝，善导引行气。历阳有彭祖仙室，前世祷请风雨，莫不辄应。常有两虎在祠左右，祠讫，地即有虎迹，云后升仙而去。

遐哉硕仙，时唯彭祖。道与化新，绵绵历古。隐伦玄室，灵著风雨。二虎啸时，莫我猜侮。

参考译文

彭祖，原为殷朝的一位大夫。他姓籛，名铿，是帝颛顼的孙子，陆终氏家族的中子，从夏朝一直活到殷朝末年，共活了八百多岁。彭祖常常食用上好的灵芝，擅长导引和行气之术。历阳地区有彭祖的仙室，以前的人在此祈求风雨，通常请求都会立即得到应允。仙室的左右常有两只虎守护，每当祭祀完毕，地面就会出现虎的踪迹。据说后来彭祖升仙离开了人间。

这位伟大的仙人，那一时代唯独彭祖。他的道与化融为一体，绵延不断地流传于古今。在隐秘的玄室中，他的灵力能够呼风唤雨。当两只虎在此怒吼时，没有人敢小觑或轻视他。

Pengzu was a high official of the Yin dynasty. His surname was Jian, and his given name was Keng. He was a grandson of Emperor Zhuanxu and the middle son of the Luzhong family. He lived for over eight hundred years, from the Xia dynasty to the end of the Yin dynasty. Pengzu often consumed fine glossy ganoderma and was skilled in the practices of guiding and circulating qi. In Liyang, there is a hermitage of Pengzu where people from previous generations prayed for wind and rain, and their prayers were invariably answered immediately. There are always two tigers guarding on either side of the hermitage; after the completion of worship, tiger tracks would appear on the ground. It is said that later Pengzu ascended to immortality and departed from the human world.

Oh, what a great immortal he was, unique in his time as Pengzu. His Tao blended seamlessly with transformation, enduring through the ages. Within the secluded and mystical chambers, his spirit had the power to summon wind and rain. When the two tigers roared, no one dared to underestimate or scorn him.

课 后练习

1. 选择题："受命于天"在商朝的语境中意味着什么？

A. 统治者的权力是从祖先继承来的。

B. 统治者被视为直接由天赋予治理的权力。

C. 统治者与其他部族领袖共享权力。

D. 统治者由人民选举产生。

2. 判断题：商朝的统治者使用占卜实践来证明他们的政治决策，声称他们的行为是由神意指导的。

3. 填空题：根据商朝的信仰完成以下陈述："商朝统治者声称他们的统治权是来自_____，这圣化了他们的统治，并将其直接与神圣领域联系起来。"

4. 简答题：根据文本解释"神权"或"天命"在维持商朝统治者权威和合法性中的重要性。

5. 讨论题：信仰天命如何影响商朝的政治和社会结构。

课 文参考翻译

The rulers of the Xia and Shang dynasties claimed that they governed by the mandate of Heaven, a divine authority bestowed upon them, which is known as "receiving the mandate from Heaven." *The Book of Documents: Decree of Shao* records: "Xia complied with the mandate of Heaven," "Yin (Shang) received the mandate of Heaven." Regarding the origin of the Shang dynasty, *The Book of Songs: Songs of Shang: The Black Bird* states: "Heaven decreed the black bird, descended to give birth to Shang." This highlights both the sanctity and the legitimacy of their rule, meaning, they ruled by the right of "Heaven's mandate." Consequently, commands issued and laws enacted by the rulers were considered expressions of divine will, beyond dispute.

In the literature and oracle bone inscriptions of the Shang dynasty, reverence for Heaven is frequently evident. For example, the oracle bone inscription on the scapula 2–2, according to academic research, is the largest complete inscription found to date. It documents divinations made over ten days, using sheep and other sacrificial offerings to carry out burning sacrifices to the ancestral Shang kings and mountain gods, inquiring about when it would rain.

Such records are abundant in oracle bone inscriptions, indicating the Shang people's worship of Heaven. Shang rulers intertwined political governance with the worship of ancestors and Heaven, suggesting that their ruling authority stemmed from arrangements made by "Heaven" or their ancestors, and was carried out according to the will of Heaven or their ancestors.

Beyond the ideology of "receiving the mandate from Heaven," rulers of the Xia and Shang also "respectfully carried out Heaven's punishments." They proclaimed their campaigns or chastisements against other tribes or opposition forces as punishments conducted according to the will of Heaven. For example, when King Qi of Xia campaigned against the Hu tribe, he declared it "respectfully carrying out Heaven's punishment" : "Heaven has decreed to eradicate their destiny, today I merely carry out Heaven's punishment," as recorded in *The Book of Documents: The Oath of Gan*.When King Tang of Shang overthrew the Xia, he did so under the banner of "Heaven," as recorded in *The Book of Documents: The Oath of Tang*: "Xia has many sins, Heaven has decreed their doom." Tang stated that because "the Xia clan has sinned," "I fear Heaven and dare not fail to act righteously." Due to his reverence for "Heaven," the campaign against Xia was "Heaven's will," making King Tang's actions "respectfully carrying out Heaven's punishment," compelling him to act.

Xia and Shang rulers' practices of "divine judgment," based on divination text to enact laws, not only commanded respect and belief among the people but also supported the ruling class in maintaining control and stability.

第三课

西周时期的法律

课 前准备

图 3-1　山西青铜博物馆：西周·青铜器及铭文

周部族有着悠长的历史，其始祖名弃，根据《史记·周本纪》的记载，弃**"好耕农，相地之宜，宜谷者稼穑焉，民皆法则之。帝尧闻之，举弃为农师，天下得其利，有功…… 封弃于邰，号曰后稷，别姓姬氏"**。之后，周人不断发展壮大，在商朝统治后期，文王姬昌被封为西伯侯。公元前 11 世纪，商王朝内部政治腐败，对外掠夺压迫，导致众叛亲离，周武王率军赢得牧野之战，推翻商朝统治，建立周朝。在周平王于公元前 770 年向东迁都洛邑之前，周朝的统治时期通称"西周"。西周是中国法律发展史和法律文明史上的重要时期，这一时期的法律思想、法律制度及国家治理的经验对后世产生重大影响。[1]

----

〔1〕 参见朱勇主编：《中国法律史》，中国政法大学出版社 2021 年版，第 22 页。

The Zhou tribe has a long history, and its progenitor was named Qi. According to *The Records of the Grand Historian: Annals of Zhou*, Qi "was skilled in agriculture, selecting suitable lands for grains, and the people followed his methods. Emperor Yao heard of this, raised Qi to the position of Minister of Agriculture, and the world benefited greatly from his contributions…Qi was ennobled in Tai and given the title Hou Ji, with the separate family name Ji." Subsequently, the Zhou people continued to grow and strengthen. During the late rule of the Shang Dynasty, King Wen of Zhou, Ji Chang, was conferred the title of Marquis of the West. In the 11th century BC, due to internal corruption and oppressive conquests leading to widespread disaffection, King Wu of Zhou led his army to victory in the Battle of Muye, overthrowing the Shang Dynasty and establishing the Zhou Dynasty. Before King Ping of Zhou moved the capital eastward to Luoyi in 770 BC, the period was known as the "Western Zhou." The Western Zhou was a significant era in the history of legal development and legal civilization in China, with its legal ideas, systems, and governance experience profoundly influencing subsequent generations.

 生词表

序号	生词	词性	汉语拼音	英文解释
1	始祖	*n.*	shǐ zǔ	ancestor
2	好耕农	*phr.*	hào gēng nóng	skilled in farming
3	相地	*phr.*	xiàng dì	survey the land
4	稼穑	*n.*	jià sè	farming and harvesting
5	法则	*n.*	fǎ zé	rule，principle
6	农师	*n.*	nóng shī	agricultural instructor
7	封	*v.*	fēng	confer a title or land
8	后稷	*proper n.*	Hòu jì	mythical ancestor
9	姬氏	*proper n.*	Jī shì	the Ji clan

续表

序号	生词	词性	汉语拼音	英文解释
10	伯侯	*n.*	bó hóu	marquis，feudal lord
11	掠夺	*v.*	lüè duó	plunder，loot
12	众叛亲离	*idm.*	zhòng pàn qīn lí	everyone forsakes one
13	牧野	*proper n.*	Mù yě	historical site
14	洛邑	*proper n.*	Luò yì	ancient city

尽管夏商的统治者都宣称自己的统治是"受命于天"，但是他们的统治最后都被推翻了。周朝人也因此认识到，仅仅依靠"天命观"并不能有力地解释为何"受命于天"的商朝统治会被自己推翻，而自己的统治也宣称是"受命于天"却有正当性。所以，周朝统治者在之前"天命""天罚"观念的基础上进一步提出"以德配天"以及"礼治"的思想原则，以此巩固并维护自己的统治。这一思想对后世的法律思想和法律制度产生了极其深远的影响。[1]

课 文

周朝的统治者在之前的天命神权思想的基础上，提出来"德"的观念和"以德配天"的思想理论，把"德"和"天命"联系起来，认为"天命"不是固定不变的，仅有"天命"和上天的眷顾并不能保证建立和维护统治，统治者必须要有"德"，才有资格"受天命"，并得到民众的拥护。在"以德配天"的基础上，西周的统治者还提出"明德慎罚"的思想，即阐明德教、谨慎刑罚的内涵。"明德慎罚"思想，一方面要求统治者"尚德"，另一方面要求统

---

〔1〕 参见朱勇主编：《中国法律史》，中国政法大学出版社 2021 年版，第 22 页。

治者谨慎刑罚，不滥杀无辜。因此可以说，"明德慎罚"思想是对"以德配天"思想的进一步发展，后世的儒家在此基础上发展成为"德主刑辅"的思想，成为中国古代治国理政的重要思想原则和经验总结。

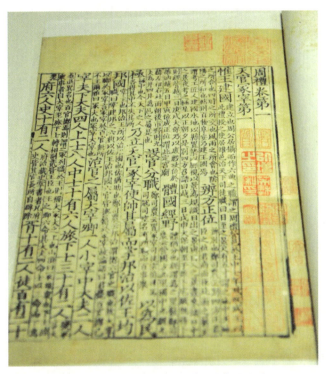

图 3-2　国家典籍博物馆：《周礼》宋刻本

除此之外，西周时期的"礼"也具有国家治理和维护社会秩序的功能。"礼"为汉字一级字，甲骨文中就有"礼"字，其意义原本跟祭祀有关，与神权法思想有着密切的联系。西周时期的"礼治"以宗法制为基础，建立在血缘关系的基础上，并且与政治关系高度一致，形成"家""国"一体的宗法政权体制。周天子作为西周的最高统治者，是天下的"大宗"，其"大宗"的身份由嫡长子继承；周天子的同姓兄弟为天下的"小宗"，被分封到各个诸侯国，但诸侯们在各自的封国中，又是封国的"大宗"；以此类推。

西周的宗法制和"礼治"的核心是"亲亲""尊尊"。《礼记·大传》记载：
"亲亲也，尊尊也，长长也，男女有别。"

与夏商时期的法律相比，西周法律在内容上具有明显的进步性，并且体现出较高的文明化程度，形成了一些较为合理的刑法原则和较为完整的刑罚体系，其"五刑"仍以"肉刑"为主，包括墨、劓、荆、宫、大辟 5 种刑罚；同时也存在一些具有劳役刑性质的其他刑罚，如"圜土"之制、"嘉石"之制，以及鞭刑、流刑等。

　　到了西周中后期，随着社会的发展，民事和经济活动进一步活跃，以调整财产关系和婚姻家庭关系为主要内容的民事法律规范得到进一步发展，并在社会生活中发挥重要作用，尤其以土地所有权的变化以及契约关系的出现最为显著。

　　在司法制度上，西周时期的诉讼制度在总结之前司法经验的基础上初步形成了一些基本的司法原则。《周礼·秋官·大司寇》记载：**"以两造禁民讼，入束矢于朝，然后听之。以两剂禁民狱，入钧金，三日乃致于朝，然后听之。"**这里的"讼"类似于民事案件，"狱"类似于刑事案件。东汉郑玄注称："讼谓以财货相告者"，"狱谓相告以罪名者"。根据一般的理解，"束矢"（即一百支箭）和"钧金"（即三十斤铜）是当时需要缴纳的诉讼费用。[1]

 生词表

序号	生词	词性	汉语拼音	英文解释
1	天命神权	*n.*	tiān mìng shén quán	divine right of kings
2	德	*n.*	dé	virtue，morality
3	配天	*phr.*	pèi tiān	match heaven
4	慎罚	*phr.*	shèn fá	administer punishment cautiously
5	尚德	*phr.*	shàng dé	value virtue
6	德主刑辅	*idm.*	dé zhǔ xíng fǔ	virtue leads and punishment supports
7	宗法制	*n.*	zōng fǎ zhì	clan system
8	大宗	*n.*	dà zōng	main branch of a family

---

〔1〕 参见朱勇主编：《中国法律史》，中国政法大学出版社 2021 年版，第 22~34 页。

续表

序号	生词	词性	汉语拼音	英文解释
9	小宗	*n.*	xiǎo zōng	secondary branch of a family
10	亲亲	*phr.*	qīn qīn	favor relatives
11	尊尊	*phr.*	zūn zūn	respect the respectable
12	墨	*n.*	mò	tattooing punishment
13	劓	*n.*	yì	nose cutting punishment
14	剕	*n.*	fèi	foot amputation punishment
15	宫	*n.*	gōng	castration punishment
16	大辟	*n.*	dà pì	death penalty
17	圜土	*n.*	yuán tǔ	prison，a type of labor punishment
18	嘉石	*n.*	jiā shí	a form of punishment or labor
19	鞭刑	*n.*	biān xíng	whipping punishment
20	流刑	*n.*	liú xíng	exile punishment
21	契约	*n.*	qì yuē	contract
22	司寇	*n.*	sī kòu	minister of justice
23	讼	*n.*	sòng	lawsuit，litigation
24	狱	*n.*	yù	prison，legal case
25	束矢	*n.*	shù shǐ	a bundle of arrows，metaphor for legal fee
26	钧金	*n.*	jūn jīn	thirty jin of metal，metaphor for legal fee

重 点汉字【刑】

在古汉字中，"刑"与"井"有密切关系。甲骨文里的"井"字主要用作人名如"妇井"或地名，并未涉及法律含义。根据姚孝遂的《殷墟甲骨刻辞类纂》，"井"在甲骨文中出现了 84 处，但都没有与法律相关的用法。进入西周时期，"井"字的用途扩展到更广泛的含义。据周法高的《金文诂林》，金文中"井"字出现 71 次，其中不少通假作"刑"，用作表达"遵循，以为楷模"的意思，部分还表达了"法律规范"的概念，如"怀刑""明刑"等，用以描述具体的法律规定和惩罚措施。到了东周，对"刑"字的使用出现了变化。"刑"字在甲骨文中未见，而在周代金文中以记载于物上的形式出现。这种写法主要集中在东周的器物上，如"中刑""中敷明刑"，都指"法律规范"。因此，总的来说，"井"是早期的本字，表铸器之范或模型之意，后来发展为表示遵循或典范的动词。随着时间的推移，"井"字衍生出"刑"字，后者逐渐具有了刑罚的含义，特别是在描述法律规范时。这种演变反映了古代文字与法律观念的密切联系，以及语言如何发展以适应社会和文化的需求。

图 3-3　"刑"字篆刻（王琦 刻）

 汉字拓展

序号	词汇	汉语拼音	英文解释	例句
1	刑法	xíng fǎ	criminal law	这个国家最近修订了它的刑法。
2	刑场	xíng chǎng	execution ground	古代的刑场通常在城外。
3	刑期	xíng qī	sentence term	他被判了五年的刑期。
4	有期徒刑	yǒu qī tú xíng	fixed-term imprisonment	他被判了三年有期徒刑。
5	刑事案件	xíng shì àn jiàn	criminal case	这个刑事案件非常复杂。

续表

序号	词汇	汉语拼音	英文解释	例句
6	刑警	xíng jǐng	criminal police	刑警迅速赶到了案发现场。
7	刑侦	xíng zhēn	criminal investigation	刑侦工作需要细致和耐心。
8	缓刑	huǎn xíng	suspended sentence	他因表现良好而被判缓刑。
9	无期徒刑	wú qī tú xíng	life imprisonment	最严重的罪行可能会判处无期徒刑。
10	轻刑	qīng xíng	light punishment	对于小罪行，法院可能会判处轻刑。
11	重刑	zhòng xíng	heavy punishment	重大犯罪通常会被处以重刑。
12	减刑	jiǎn xíng	sentence reduction	他因为在狱中表现好而获得了减刑。
13	刑事诉讼	xíng shì sù sòng	criminal litigation	刑事诉讼程序通常较为严格。

文 化知识【龙之九子】

图 3-4　中国考古博物馆：西汉·青龙纹瓦当

图 3-5　北京银山塔林：钟亭

图 3-6　中国考古博物馆：石螭首

　　中国古代神话传说中，和法律有关的动物形象除了獬豸，还有狴犴，其是龙的九个儿子中的一个。

　　关于中国的龙到底长什么样，说法五花八门。明朝宰相李东阳的《怀麓堂集》里面记载，龙一共有九个儿子，所谓"龙生九子，各不相同"：

长子囚牛，喜欢音乐，住在胡琴头上。

二子睚眦，喜欢打架，经常被刻在武器上。

三子嘲风，喜欢探险和高望，所以挺立在屋顶垂脊。

四子蒲牢，声音洪亮，常作为古时铜钟的兽钮（见图 3-5）。

五子狻猊，喜欢烟火，常坐在寺庙的香炉炉角。

六子霸下，身形似龟、头却似龙，曾在上古时期驮着三山五岳。

七子狴犴，似虎，好讼。是法兽，看监狱、守公堂。

八子负屃。霸下好负重，负屃好文。所以，霸下在碑下，负屃在碑上，他们常常成组出现。

九子螭吻（鸱吻），又叫龙形吞脊兽，五行属水，镇邪避火。一般是大殿正脊两端的卷尾龙头，有时背插一个剑柄（见图 3-6）。

法 治文物【"獬豸"博物馆（三）】

图 3-7　东汉·青铜独角兽[1]

---

〔1〕参见李雪梅：《谜一样的独角兽（一）》，载《中国法律评论》2021 年第 2 期。

经 典阅读

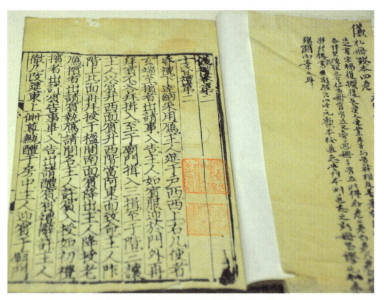

图 3-8　国家典籍博物馆：仪礼残卷 元刻本

　　《礼记·昏义》[1]：昏礼者，将合二姓之好，上以事宗庙，而下以继后世也，故君子重之。是以昏礼纳采、问名、纳吉、纳征、请期，皆主人筵几于庙，而拜迎于门外，入，揖让而升，听命于庙，所以敬慎重正昏礼也。

　　父亲醮子而命之迎，男先于女也。子承命以迎，主人筵几于庙，而拜迎于门外。婿执雁入，揖让升堂，再拜奠雁，盖亲受之于父母也。降出，御妇车，而婿授绥，御轮三周，先俟于门外。妇至，婿揖妇以入，共牢而食，合卺而酳，所以合体同尊卑以亲之也。

　　敬慎重正而后亲之，礼之大体，而所以成男女之别，而立夫妇之义也。男女有别，而后夫妇有义；夫妇有义，而后父子有亲；父子有亲，而后君臣有正。故曰："昏礼者，礼之本也。"

_____

　　〔1〕　选自王文锦译解：《礼记译解》，中华书局 2016 年版，第 820~821 页。

参考译文

婚礼的礼仪，是为了联合两个家族，通过举行庄重的婚礼来祭祀祖先并继承家族血脉，因此君子非常重视这个仪式。婚礼包括多个环节：纳采（男方向女方提亲）、问名（询问女方姓名）、纳吉（择吉日向女方告知）、纳征（支付聘金）、请期（确定婚期）。这些环节都在家庙中主持，新郎在门外迎接新娘，两人在庙中接受祖先的见证，展现婚礼的庄严和重视。

婚礼流程是：父亲为儿子敬酒，并命令儿子去迎接新娘。婚礼在家庙中举行，新郎在门外等候。新郎持雁（大雁代表忠贞）进入，向新娘鞠躬后一同进入家庙，再次鞠躬并将雁奠下，象征受父母之命而结合。接着，新郎下堂，出门，驾着新娘乘坐的车子，将登车的挽绳交于新娘，再驾车让车轮转动三圈，然后将车子交给车夫驾驶，自己回到家门外等候。新娘到了以后，新郎作揖迎接新娘，然后一同进入家门。之后，夫妇共同进行祭祀，共享食物，喝交杯酒，表示双方的结合和相互尊重。

先互相敬重然后发展亲密关系，这是礼最重要的内容，也是男女有别、然后有夫妻情义的原因。先男女有别，而后夫妻之间才能有情义；夫妻有情有义，才能有父子亲情；父子之间有亲情，君臣关系才能规范而符合标准。所以说："婚礼是礼的基础。"

The rituals of marriage are designed to unite two families, sacrifice ancestors, and continue the family lineage through the solemn ceremony of marriage. Thus, gentlemen place great importance on this ritual. The marriage ceremony includes several stages: "纳采" (the proposal by the groom's family), "问名" (inquiring about the bride's name), "纳吉" (choosing an auspicious date and informing the bride's family), "纳征" (paying the bride price), and "请期" (setting the wedding date). These stages are conducted in the ancestral temple. The groom waits outside to welcome the bride, and together they receive the witness of their ancestors in the temple, displaying the solemnity and respect of the wedding.

The wedding process is as follows：The father propose a toast for his son and instructs the son to welcome the bride. The wedding is held in the ancestral temple, with the groom waiting outside. The groom, holding a wild goose (goose symbolizing fidelity), enters the temple, bows to the bride, and then they enter the temple together, bow again, and place the wild goose on the altar, symbolizing their union under the command of their parents. Next, the groom leaves the temple and goes out, handing the rope of the car to the bride and driving the bride's car. When the car's wheel has turned three times, the groom lets the coachman drive the car then he goes first and waits outside his house. When the bride arrives, the groom greets her with a bow, and then they enter the family home together. Afterward, the couple performs a sacrifice, shares food, and drinks wine, symbolizing their union and mutual respect.

Respecting each other first and then developing intimacy is the core content of the rites, which explains the reason for the differentiation between men and women, leading to the affection between husband and wife. The distinction between men and women is followed by the affection and righteousness between husband and wife; when there is affection between husband and wife, there can be parental affection; when there is parental affection, the relationship between ruler and subject can be regulated and conform to standards. Therefore, it is said, "The marriage rites are the foundation of all rites."

课 后练习

1. 选择题：根据文章，以下哪些观念是周朝统治者特别重视的？

A. 以德配天

B. 明德慎罚

C. 德主刑辅

D. 礼治宗法

2.判断题：在西周时期，"礼"主要指的是与神权法思想相关的祭祀活动。

3.填空题：在西周时期，统治者把"＿＿＿＿＿＿"和"天命"联系起来，认为统治者必须要有"＿＿＿＿＿＿"才有资格"受天命"。

4.简答题：请描述"明德慎罚"思想的主要内容和它对后世儒家思想的影响。

5.讨论题：西周的宗法制和"礼治"如何维护社会秩序和政治稳定。请提供具体的历史背景和制度细节以支持你的观点。

课 文参考翻译

The rulers of the Zhou dynasty, building on the earlier divine mandate concept, introduced the notion of "virtue" and the theoretical framework of "matching heaven with virtue." They connected "virtue" with "heavenly mandate," believing that the mandate was not fixed and unchangeable. Simply possessing the mandate and the favor of heaven did not guarantee the establishment and maintenance of rule; rulers needed to possess "virtue" to qualify for the "heavenly mandate" and to gain the support of the people. Based on the principle of "matching heaven with virtue," the Western Zhou rulers also advocated the idea of "illuminating virtue and being cautious in punishment," which meant clarifying the teaching of virtue and being prudent with punishments. This idea, emphasizing the importance for rulers to value virtue and be cautious about administering capital punishment, represented a further development of the "matching heaven with virtue" concept. Later Confucianism developed this into the idea of "virtue as the mainstay and punishment as the support," forming an essential ideological and experiential principle for ancient Chinese governance.

Additionally, during the Western Zhou period, the concept of "ritual" played a significant role in state governance and social order maintenance. "Ritual" was a first-level character in Chinese, with origins in oracle bone inscriptions closely linked to divine law. The "ritual governance" of the Western Zhou, based on clan systems, was highly consistent with political relationships, establishing a governance system that integrated family and state. The Zhou king, as the supreme ruler, was considered the "great lineage," a role inherited by his eldest legitimate son; his brothers, sharing the same surname, were "lesser lineages" and were enfeoffed in various vassal states, where they were the "great lineages" within their domains.

The core of Western Zhou's clan system and ritual governance was the principle of "respecting kin and honoring the noble." *The Book of Rites: Great Commentary* records, "to respect kin, to honor the noble, to prioritize the elder, and to distinguish between male and female."

Compared to the legal systems of the Xia and Shang periods, Western Zhou laws showed significant progress and a higher degree of civilization, forming more rational penal principles and a more complete penal system. The "Five Punishments," still primarily corporeal, included tattooing, amputation of the nose, foot amputation, castration, and the death penalty. There were also labor-related penalties such as "encircling land" and "carrying stones," along with whipping and exile.

In the mid-to-late Western Zhou period, as society developed and civil and economic activities became more vibrant, civil laws, mainly concerning property relations and family matters, evolved further and played a crucial role in social life, especially noticeable in changes to land ownership and the emergence of contractual relationships.

In terms of judicial systems, the Western Zhou litigation system began to form basic judicial principles based on previous experiences. *The Rites of Zhou: Autumn Officials: Major Judge* records, "For civil disputes, litigants must deposit a bundle of arrows at court, then the case may be heard. For criminal cases, they must deposit thirty jin of metal and wait three days before being admitted to court for a hearing." Here, "讼" is similar to civil cases, and "狱" to criminal cases. According to Zheng Xuan's annotation in the Eastern Han, "讼 refers to disputes over property," and "狱 refers to accusations of criminal offenses." The required litigation fees were a bundle of arrows (one hundred arrows) and thirty jin of metal.

第四课

春秋战国时期的法律

课 前准备

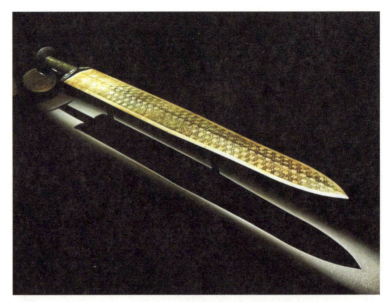

图 4-1　湖北省博物馆：春秋·越王勾践剑

　　公元前 770 年，周平王向东迁都洛邑，开始了中国历史上 500 余年的春秋战国时期。在春秋时期，虽然周王室衰微，"礼崩乐坏"，但是周天子在名义上仍是"天下共主"，列国在攻伐时，仍然打着"尊王攘夷"的旗号；然而，战国时期，各国更为直接地**"争于气力"**（《韩非子·五蠹》），为求富国强兵而纷纷实行变法，战争更是各国不得不面对的事情。在春秋战国时期，社会动荡，制度变革，旧的政治、经济、社会制度已经不适应当时的情势，政治、经济、社会关系发生巨大变化。在当时的时代背景下，不仅思想文化领域出现了"百家争鸣"的局面，各国法律制度也处于不断的变革发展之中。

　　法家思想最早从春秋初期的齐国管仲和郑国子产开始，实际创始者是战国前期的李悝、商鞅、慎到、申不害等。而法家思想最重要的代表人物，则是战国末期的韩国人韩非，他建立了完整的法治理论。韩非子的老师出自儒家，但韩非却反对儒家的"礼制"，强调法的"定分止争"，继承并发展了法家思想，把"法""术""势"完美结合，最终成为法家集大成者。他的著作《韩非子》广为流传，书中记载了大量寓言故事，如"自相矛盾""守株待兔""讳疾忌医""滥竽充数""老马识途"，等等。[1]

In 770 BC, King Ping of Zhou moved the capital east to Luoyi, marking the beginning of the Spring and Autumn Period and Warring States Period that lasted over 500 years in Chinese history. During the Spring and Autumn Period, despite the decline of the Zhou royal house and the decay of rites and music, the Zhou Emperor was still nominally the "common sovereign" of the world, and states during their conquests still rallied under the banner of "honoring the king and expelling the barbarians." However, during the Warring States Period, states competed in "struggles of power" (as described in *Han Feizi: Wudu*), adopting various reforms to strengthen their nations and armies, making war an inevitable affair. This era was marked by social turmoil, systemic changes, and the old political, economic, and social systems no longer being suitable for the times, leading to significant transformations in political, economic, and social relations. This period also witnessed the "Contention of a Hundred Schools of Thought" and significant reforms in legal systems.

Legalist thought began in the early Spring and Autumn Period with figures like Guan Zhong of Qi and Zi Chan of Zheng, with its foundational developments occurring in the early Warring States Period through figures like Li Kui, Shang Yang, Shen Dao, and Shen Buhai. The most significant proponent of Legalism was Han Fei from the state of Han towards the end of the Warring States Period, who established a complete theory of legalism. Although Han Fei's teacher came from the Confucian school, Han Fei himself opposed the Confucian ritual system, emphasizing the role of law in "determining roles and resolving conflicts." He developed Legal-

---

〔1〕　参见朱勇主编:《中国法律史》，中国政法大学出版社 2021 年版，第 35~60 页。

ism further, perfectly integrating "law," "tactic," and "power," culminating in the synthesis of Legalist thought. His works, collected in *Han Feizi*, include many parables such as "The Self-Contradicting Spear and Shield," "Waiting for a Hare by a Stump," "Concealing Illness," "Filling the Ranks with Mediocre Musicians," "The Old Horse Knows the Way," and so on.

 生词表

序号	生词	词性	汉语拼音	英文解释
1	衰微	*adj.*	shuāi wēi	declined, weak
2	礼崩乐坏	*idm.*	lǐ bēng yuè huài	collapse of rites and music（chaos）
3	天下共主	*n.*	tiān xià gòng zhǔ	ruler of all under heaven
4	尊王攘夷	*idm.*	zūn wáng rǎng yí	honor the king and repel the barbarians
5	争于气力	*idm.*	zhēng yú qì lì	struggle for power and strength
6	变法	*n.*	biàn fǎ	political reform
7	争鸣	*v.*	zhēng míng	contend vocally, debate
8	管仲	*proper n.*	Guǎn Zhòng	famous strategist
9	子产	*proper n.*	Zǐ chǎn	statesman of Zheng
10	定分止争	*idm.*	dìng fēn zhǐ zhēng	define roles to prevent disputes
11	韩非	*proper n.*	Hán Fēi	legalist philosopher
12	寓言	*n.*	yù yán	fable, parable

 导 读

　　春秋战国时期，随着社会生产力的发展和社会结构的变化，政治、经济、法律制度经历了重大的转型和变革，人们对政治、经济、社会的看法也发生了根本性的变化。首先，经济迅速发展，社会结构发生变化。冶铁技术的进步和铁制工具的广泛使用促进了土地的开垦和农业技术的提升，大大提高了生产效率和农业产量，推动了经济的快速发展和社会生产方式的变革。与此同时，田地私有化现象增多，传统的井田制逐渐瓦解，新的社会阶层如地主、农民及工商业者等应运而生，社会阶级结构发生显著变动。其次，随着周王室权力衰微，基于血缘的宗法制和分封制受到冲击，诸侯国力量增强，"礼乐征伐"的权力从天子转至诸侯，形成了诸侯争霸的局面。据《史记》记载，春秋期间弑君和亡国事件频发，表明旧有政治体制和治理方式已不适应新的社会需求，众多国家的土地、税制、官制和法律体系均经历了改革。这一时期的变革标志着从"礼治"向"法治"的转变。此外，文化层面上，春秋战国时期也是思想文化大发展的时期，各种学派如儒家、法家、墨家、道家、阴阳家等纷纷兴起，形成了所谓的"百家争鸣"。这些学派就如何在社会动荡中寻求国家发展和强化国力提出了各种理论和建议，极大丰富了中国的哲学和政治思想。

课　文

荆庄王制定了一项法令，称为"茅门之法"，规定："大臣和公子入朝时，若马蹄踩到屋檐下面滴水之处，宫廷管理者应斩断其车辕并处决车夫。"因此，当太子入朝时，他的马蹄踩到了檐下滴水之处，宫廷管理者依法斩断了他的车辕并杀了他的车夫。太子非常愤怒，进入宫廷哭着对庄王说："请为我处决那位宫廷管理者。"庄王回答说："法律是用来尊重宗庙和崇高社稷的。因此，那些能够制定法律并且遵守、尊敬社稷的人是社稷的良臣，怎么能被处死呢？而那些犯法废弃命令、不尊重社稷的人，他们是在凌驾于君上，是下位者侵犯上位者。如果臣子凌驾于君上，那么国王就会失去威严；如果下位者试图取代上位者，那么上位者就处于危险之中。失去威严、危及君位，社稷将无法守护。我还能把什么传给子孙后代呢？"于是太子退回，避开房屋露宿三天，面朝北方跪拜请求死罪。

图 4-2　湖北省博物馆：战国·曾侯乙尊盘

　　另一种说法是，楚庄王（即前文荆庄王）急切召见太子。按照楚国的法律，车辆不得行至茆门。那天下雨，院中有积水，太子便驱车直至茆门。宫廷管理者说："车辆不得开到茆门，这是违法的。"太子回答："国王召唤急迫，不能因为积水而延误。"太子继续驾车前进。于是宫廷管理者举起武器击打太子的马，破坏了他的车辆。太子进宫哭着对国王说："庭中有很多积水，所以我驱车至茆门，宫廷管理者说这是违法的，并用武器击打我的马，毁了我的车辆。父王必须杀了他。"庄王说："他是前有老主而不越界，后有储主而不附和，值得表扬！他确实是我坚守法律的臣子。"于是庄王提升了这名宫廷管理者的爵位两级，并打开后门让太子离开，告诉他以后不要再犯这样的错误。

 原文参考

　　《韩非子·外储说右上》：荆庄王有茆门之法曰："群臣大夫诸公子入朝，

马蹄践霤者，廷理斩其辀戮其御。"于是太子入朝，马蹄践霤，廷理斩其辀，戮其御。太子怒，入为王泣曰："为我诛戮廷理。"王曰："法者，所以敬宗庙，尊社稷。故能立法从令尊敬社稷者，社稷之臣也，焉可诛也？夫犯法废令不尊敬社稷者，是臣乘君而下尚校也。臣乘君，则主失威；下尚校，则上位危。威失位危，社稷不守，吾将何以遗子孙？"于是太子乃还走，避舍露宿三日，北面再拜请死罪。

一曰：楚王急召太子。楚国之法，车不得至于茆门。天雨，廷中有潦，太子遂驱车至于茆门。廷理曰："车不得至茆门。非法也。"太子曰："王召急，不得须无潦。"遂驱之。廷理举殳而击其马，败其驾。太子入为王泣曰："廷中多潦，驱车至茆门，廷理曰'非法也'，举殳击臣马，败臣驾。王必诛之。"王曰："前有老主而不逾，后有储主而不属，矜矣！是直吾守法之臣也。"乃益爵二级，而开后门出太子。勿复过。

 ### 生词表

序号	生词	词性	汉语拼音	英文解释
1	荆庄王	*proper n.*	Jīng zhuāng wáng	King Zhuang of Jing
2	茅门之法	*proper n.*	Máo mén zhī fǎ	a law to guarantee the safety of the king
3	入朝	*phr.*	rù cháo	attend court
4	马蹄	*n.*	mǎ tí	horse's hoof
5	处决	*v.*	chǔ jué	execute
6	宫廷管理者	*n.*	gōng tíng guǎn lǐ zhě	court administrator
7	斩杀	*v.*	zhǎn shā	behead, kill
8	宗庙	*n.*	zōng miào	ancestral temple
9	社稷	*n.*	shè jì	national altar（sovereignty）

续表

序号	生词	词性	汉语拼音	英文解释
10	凌驾	v.	líng jià	override
11	臣子	n.	chén zǐ	subject，minister
12	威严	n.	wēi yán	dignity，majesty
13	上位者	n.	shàng wèi zhě	those in superior positions
14	下位者	n.	xià wèi zhě	those in inferior positions
15	守护	v.	shǒu hù	guard，protect
16	避舍	v.	bì shè	take shelter
17	露宿	v.	lù sù	sleep outdoors
18	请死罪	phr.	qǐng sǐ zuì	request punishment for death
19	积水	n.	jī shuǐ	accumulated water，puddle
20	驱车	phr.	qū chē	drive a chariot
21	举殳	phr.	jǔ shū	raise a weapon
22	越界	v.	yuè jiè	overstep boundaries
23	储主	n.	chǔ zhǔ	crown prince，heir apparent
24	爵位	n.	jué wèi	noble rank
25	后门	n.	hòu mén	back door

重 点汉字【罪】

　　"罪"，古时也写做"辠"，从自从辛，"自"表示鼻子，"辛"通说为一种刑具，即"辠"用劓刑表示有罪。后来字形演变，"罪"变为会意字，指捕鱼用的竹网。秦始皇把"辠"改为会意字"罪"，据说是因为秦始皇认为"辠"字与"皇"字相似，因此将其改为"罪"。在秦朝以后的经典中，"辠"经常写作"罪"；且在竹简和丝帛文献中，"罪"用于本义"捕鱼竹网"的情况很少见。《诗经·小雅》："畏此罪罟"，《诗经·大雅》："天降罪罟"，这里的"罪罟"都表示"罪网"。

图 4-3　"罪"字篆刻（王琦 刻）

　汉字拓展

序号	词汇	汉语拼音	英文解释	例句
1	罪行	zuì xíng	crime	他因为严重的罪行被捕。
2	罪犯	zuì fàn	criminal	警方迅速逮捕了这名罪犯。
3	罪证	zuì zhèng	incriminating evidence	警方找到了确凿的罪证。
4	罪名	zuì míng	charge，accusation	他被控以多项罪名。
5	有罪	yǒu zuì	guilty	经审理，被告被判有罪。
6	无罪	wú zuì	innocent	经过调查，他被证明无罪。
7	罪责	zuì zé	guilt，responsibility	他企图逃脱罪责。
8	轻罪	qīng zuì	minor offense	法院认为这是一个轻罪。
9	罪孽	zuì niè	sin，evil deed	他为自己的罪孽深感懊悔。
10	犯罪嫌疑	fàn zuì xián yí	suspicion of crime	他因有犯罪嫌疑被警方调查。
11	罪证确凿	zuì zhèng què záo	conclusive evidence	他的罪证确凿，无法否认。
12	罪不容诛	zuì bù róng zhū	even death can not atone for the offense	此人极其残忍，罪不容诛！

文 化知识【韩非与《韩非子》】

法家思想起源于春秋初期的齐国管仲和郑国子产，实际创始人是战国前期的李悝、商鞅、慎到、申不害等，而集大成者是战国末期的韩非。韩非建立了完整的法治理论和朴素唯物主义哲学体系。据说韩非口吃，不善言谈，但其文章气势逼人，曾与李斯同为荀子的学生。韩非的思想与大儒荀子不同，他喜欢刑名法术的学说，主张清简无为的治理。

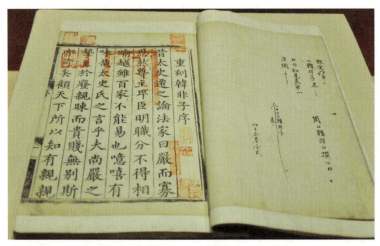

图4-4　国家典籍博物馆：《韩非子二十卷》
明万历周孔教列本"四库底本"王仁俊、黄彭年题识

韩非的著作在其本国韩国不受重视，但其思想在秦国得到高度赞赏。秦王嬴政读了他的《孤愤》和《五蠹》后，极为推崇。后来，韩非被派往秦国出使，但秦王未予信任和重用。因上书建议秦王先伐赵后伐韩，韩非受到李斯和姚贾的诋毁，并被秦王下令监禁。李斯后派人给他送毒药，迫使其自杀。尽管秦王最终后悔并下令赦免韩非，但为时已晚。

《韩非子》一书强调法、术、势的结合，成为先秦法家理论的最高峰，为秦统一六国和后来的封建专制制度提供了理论支撑。韩非还提出了矛盾学说，用矛与盾的寓言故事阐明其道理。《韩非子》中还记载了众多脍炙人口的寓言故事，如"自相矛盾""守株待兔"等，这些故事不仅富含哲理，还具有极高的文学价值，为人们提供了智慧的启迪。

 治文物【"獬豸"博物馆（四）】

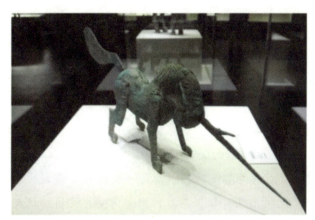

图 4-5　魏晋·青铜神兽[1]

经 典阅读

《韩非子·说难》：昔者郑武公欲伐胡，故先以其女妻胡君以娱其意。因问于群臣："吾欲用兵，谁可伐者？"大夫关其思对曰："胡可伐。"武公怒而戮之，曰："胡，兄弟之国也，子言伐之，何也？"胡君闻之，以郑为亲己，遂不备郑，郑人袭胡，取之。

宋有富人，天雨墙坏，其子曰："不筑，必将有盗。"其邻人之父亦云。暮而果大亡其财，其家甚智其子，而疑邻人之父。

此二人说者皆当矣，厚者为戮，薄者见疑，则非知之难也，处知则难也。故绕朝之言当矣，其为圣人于晋，而为戮于秦也。此不可不察。

---

〔1〕 参见李雪梅：《谜一样的独角兽（一）》，载《中国法律评论》2021 年第 2 期。

参考译文

昔日，郑武公想要攻打胡国，因此先将自己的女儿嫁给胡国的君主，以取悦他。随后，他问群臣："我想用兵，有哪个国家可以攻打？"大夫关其思回答说："可以攻打胡国。"武公因此愤怒并处死了关其思，说道："胡国是我们的兄弟之邦，你为何说要攻打它？"胡国的君主听说了这件事，认为郑国与他亲近，便没有对郑国保持警惕。结果，郑国突袭了胡国并且获得了胜利。

宋国有一个富裕的家庭，一次下雨导致他们家的墙壁坏了，儿子说："如果不修理，一定会有小偷。"他们的邻居的父亲也这么说。到了晚上，这户人家果然发生了大失窃事件，他们家失去了许多财物。这家人非常赞赏他们的儿子的聪明，却怀疑邻居的父亲。

这两个建议者的意见都是对的，但是一个因直言遭到处死，一个因说中事而受到怀疑，说明了拥有知识不难，但如何妥善运用知识却很难。所以，即使在朝廷中的建议是正确的，在晋国可能被认为是圣人的智慧，在秦国却可能因此被处死。这是一个不容忽视的教训。

In the past, Duke Wu of Zheng wanted to attack the state of Hu. Therefore, he first married his daughter to the ruler of Hu to please him. Afterwards, he asked his ministers, "I want to use military force. Which country can we attack?" The minister Guan Qisi answered, "We can attack Hu." Duke Wu became angry and executed Guan Qisi, saying, "Hu is a fraternal state to us. Why do you suggest attacking it?" When the ruler of Hu heard about this, he believed that Zheng was friendly towards him and did not stay vigilant against Zheng. As a result, Zheng launched a surprise attack on Hu and was victorious.

In the state of Song, there was a wealthy family whose wall was damaged by rain. The son said, "If we do not repair it, there will surely be thieves." A father of their neighbors said the same. By evening, indeed, a major theft occurred, and the family lost much of their wealth. The family greatly admired their son's intelligence but suspected the neighbor's father.

Both advisers were correct, but one was executed for his frankness, and the other was suspected for his accurate prediction, demonstrating that possessing knowledge is not difficult, but applying it wisely is. Therefore, even if advice is correct in the royal court, what might be considered wise in the state of Jin could lead to execution in Qin. This is a lesson that should not be overlooked.

课 后练习

1.选择题：以下关于"茅门之法"的描述哪项是正确的？

A. 所有进入朝廷的车辆如果马蹄踩到滴水的地方都会被处罚。

B. 只有大臣和公子入朝时，他们车辆的马蹄踩到屋檐下滴水的地方时才会被处罚。

C. 太子入朝时触犯了法律，但是由于他的特殊身份，宫廷管理者没有采取任何行动。

D. "茅门之法"专门针对车夫和驾驶员，不涉及其他官员。

2.判断题：根据课文内容，太子因为宫廷管理者执行了"茅门之法"而请求将其处死，这一请求被国王拒绝了。

3.填空题：在荆庄王的回答中，他强调法律的作用是尊重宗庙和_____，并指出只有_____法律的人才能被视为国家的忠实臣子。

4.简答题：解释为什么荆庄王听说宫廷管理者毁坏了太子的马车时，反而奖励了宫廷管理者而非惩罚？

5.讨论题：根据荆庄王对待太子和宫廷管理者的方式，探讨楚王在维护法律和权威方面的策略及其对国家治理的影响。

课 文参考翻译

King Zhuang of Jing established a law called the "Mao Gate Law," which stipulated: "When ministers and princes enter the court, if their horse's hooves reach under the eaves, the palace administrator would cut off the shafts and put the coachman to death." Consequently, when the crown prince entered the court, his horse's hooves reached under the eaves, and the palace administrator, following the law, cut off the shafts and executed the coachman. The crown prince was furious and tearfully pleaded with the king, "Please execute that palace administrator for me." The king replied, "The law exists to respect the ancestral temples and the state's altars. Therefore, those who can establish laws and honor the altars are the true servants of the state and cannot be executed. However, those who break the law, discard orders, and disrespect the altars are overstepping their bounds and trying to replace their superiors. If ministers overstep their bounds, the king loses his authority; if subordinates try to replace their superiors, the superiors are put in danger. Without authority and order, the state cannot be preserved. Then, what do I have left for future generations?" Hence the crown prince retreated, stay away from the house, and spent three days kneeling and facing north, begging for death sentence.

Another way to put it is, the King of Chu, also known as King Zhuang of Jing mentioned above, urgently summoned the crown prince. According to Chu state law, carriages were not allowed to approach the Mao Gate. It was raining that day, and the courtyard was flooded. The crown prince drove his carriage straight to the Mao Gate. The palace administrator said, "It is against the law for carriages to approach the Mao Gate." The crown prince replied, "The king's summons is urgent, and I cannot delay because of the flood." The crown prince then proceeded to drive forward. Hence the palace administrator raised his weapon and struck the crown prince's horse, damaging the carriage. The crown prince tearfully reported to the king, "The courtyard was flooded, so I drove my carriage to the Mao Gate. The palace administrator said it was illegal, struck my horse with a weapon, and damaged my carriage. You must punish him." The king responded, "He served the previous ruler without overstepping and now serves the heir without flattering, deserving praise! He is indeed a servant of the law." The king then promoted the administrator by two ranks and allowed the crown prince to leave through the back door, instructing him not to repeat such mistakes in the future.

第五课

秦朝时期的法律

（课）前准备

图 5-1　国家典籍博物馆：里耶秦简

公元前 221 年，秦国军队在大将王贲的率领下进入不战而降的齐国都城临淄，标志着诸侯割据称雄 250 余年的战国时代的结束。在中国土地上出现了一个空前统一的、中央集权的君主专制王朝——秦帝国，昔日的秦王成为中国的"始皇帝"，史称"秦始皇"。秦统一之初，为了巩固帝国的统治，统治者采取了许多措施，包括建立以皇帝为首的**"海内为郡县，法令由一统"**

（《史记·秦始皇本纪》）的专制主义中央集权制度。在政治方面，统一的政治体制被建立起来，在中央设"三公"，即丞相、太尉、御史大夫，下设诸卿，各司其职；在地方上推行郡县制，划天下为36郡。在经济方面，统一货币和度量衡，确立封建土地私有制，并实行重农抑商政策。在思想文化方面，统一文字，"焚书坑儒"。此外，秦统治者充分运用法律的权威，奉行"法令出一"，统一战国时期各国法律条文中不尽相同的规定，在秦国原有法律基础上，重新修订，颁行全国。皇帝诏令成为具有最高法律效力和最基本的法律渊源。法家的"法治"原则成为立法、司法的思想基础。秦王朝以严密的法条，加强对统一后社会的专制主义统治：从人到牛马，从生产到生活，从行动到思想，强制全国人民无条件遵守帝国新的法律，《史记·秦始皇本纪》中形容为**"端平法度，万物之纪"**。

秦始皇之后，其子胡亥继位。秦二世胡亥在位时，暴虐无道，残酷剥削压迫民众，终于激起民变。公元前206年，在农民起义的烈火中，秦王朝灭亡了。[1]

In 221 BC, under the leadership of General Wang Ben, the Qin army entered Linzi, the capital city of Qi, which surrendered without a fight, marking the end of the Warring States Period that lasted over 250 years. This ushered in an era of unprecedented unification under a centralized autocratic monarchy—the Qin Empire—with the former King of Qin becoming China's "First Emperor," known historically as "Qin Shihuang." At the beginning of its unification, to solidify its rule, the regime implemented several measures, including establishing a despotic, centralized system where "all the country was divided into counties and governed by a single law" (*The Records of the Grand Historian: Qin Shihuang's Annal*). Politically, a unified government structure was set up with three chief ministers at the center—Chancellor, Grand Commandant, and Imperial Secretary—below whom various officials were appointed to

---

〔1〕　参见朱勇主编：《中国法律史》，中国政法大学出版社2021年版，第67~90页。

manage different domains. Regionally, the empire was divided into 36 counties. Economically, the currency and measures were standardized, a feudal land ownership system was established, and a policy favoring agriculture over commerce was adopted. In the realm of thought and culture, the script was standardized, and the infamous policy of "burning of books and burying of Confucianism scholars" was implemented. Moreover, the Qin rulers fully utilized the authority of the law, enforcing a unified code that rectified discrepancies in laws from the Warring States Period, based on Qin's legal foundations, and enacted nationwide. Imperial edicts became the highest legal authority and the fundamental source of law. The Legalist principle of "rule by law" became the foundation for legislative and judicial thoughts, tightening autocratic rule over the unified society. From people to livestock, from production to lifestyle, from actions to thoughts, all were compelled to unconditionally adhere to the empire's new laws, described in *The Records of the Grand Historian: Qin Shihuang's Annal* as "establishing fair measures, a standard for all under heaven."

Following Qin Shihuang, his son Huhai succeeded him. Known as Second Emperor of Qin Dynasty, the tyrannical and oppressive reign of Huhai ultimately incited a massive peasant revolt. In 206 BC, amidst the fierce flames of this uprising, the Qin dynasty was overthrown.

 生词表

序号	生词	词性	汉语拼音	英文解释
1	割据	*v.*	gē jù	rule over separate territories
2	称雄	*v.*	chēng xióng	claim hegemony
3	中央集权	*n.*	zhōng yāng jí quán	centralization of power
4	君主专制	*n.*	jūn zhǔ zhuān zhì	autocracy, absolute monarchy
5	丞相	*n.*	chéng xiàng	prime minister

续表

序号	生词	词性	汉语拼音	英文解释
6	太尉	n.	tài wèi	grand commandant
7	御史大夫	n.	yù shǐ dà fū	imperial censor
8	郡县制	n.	jùn xiàn zhì	system of prefectures and counties
9	重农抑商	idm.	zhòng nóng yì shāng	prioritize agriculture over commerce
10	焚书坑儒	idm.	fén shū kēng rú	burning of books and burying of Confucianism scholars
11	法治	n.	fǎ zhì	rule of law
12	专制主义	n.	zhuān zhì zhǔ yì	totalitarianism
13	暴虐无道	idm.	bào nüè wú dào	tyrannical and unjust
14	剥削	v.	bō xuē	exploit
15	农民起义	n.	nóng mín qǐ yì	peasant uprising

导 读

　　春秋战国时期，中国社会各方面都产生了巨大的变革。经济上，铁制农具与牛耕的应用大大提高了社会生产力，井田制走向瓦解，小农经济日趋重要，也为各国的兼并战争奠定了经济基础。社会经济的变革进而引发了政治结构的变动。政治上，春秋以来"礼崩乐坏"（《论语·季氏》），卿大夫群体在国家政权中的地位日益提高，甚至完全掌握国家政权。为了在争霸战争中取得优势，各国诸侯、卿大夫纷纷变法图强，以实现"富国强兵"的目标。在变法过程中，原有的世卿世禄制逐渐被打破，新的官僚体制逐渐确立，各国初步建立起君主专制的中央集权制度。教育上，私学兴起，教育由"学在官府"发展为"学在民间"，打破了贵族阶层对文化教育的垄断。同时，"士"阶层崛起，他们到处游说、著书立说，成为这一时期最为活跃的社会阶层。

　　这种剧变反映到思想文化领域，即出现了诸子"百家争鸣"的学术思想热潮。私学兴起、教育下移使得平民开始有机会接受教育，文化知识迅速散布到社会各阶层，为百家争鸣提供了人才基础。从春秋末期到战国初期，出现了主张"道法自然""无为而治"的老子，提倡"仁爱""礼治"的孔子，"贵虚"的列子，主张"轻物重生"的杨朱，倡导"兼爱""非攻"的墨子，倡导法治的李悝，等等。到了战国中期，出现了主张实行"王道""仁政"的孟子，主张"逍遥""齐物"的庄子，重"势"的法家慎到、重"术"的法家申不害，等等。后来，则出现了荀子、韩非等"集大成"式的学者。为了实现自身的政治理想，确保自身的学术地位，各学派之间展开了激烈的论战与交锋，同时也推动了思想文化的多元发展与繁荣。[1]

课 文

在春秋战国时期的各种思想中，法家思想对社会变革的影响最大，李悝在魏国变法、申不害在韩国变法、吴起在楚国变法，皆以法家思想为主导。而秦国地处偏僻，受中原文化影响较小，为法家思想的推行提供了社会基础。

自商鞅变法以来，法家的政治理论和法律思想一直在秦国的政治和法制建设中起着重要的指导作用。商鞅变法的成功和秦国的迅速繁荣，进一步巩固了法家理论在秦国上层建筑中的地位。无论是在统一前还是在统一后，法家的"法治"主张和重刑策略都是秦统治者的指导思想。在长期的政治实践中，秦统治者把法家的理论运用到实际政治中，形成了一系列法制建设的指导性方针。

秦统一后，统治者继续贯彻法家思想的统治地位，在继续贯彻严刑峻法的同时，采取一系列极端手段打压诸子学说在民间的发展与传播。秦始皇曾颁布《挟书律》，并下令除史官所作"秦纪"及医药、卜巫、种树等相关书籍以外，各诸侯国史书及民间所藏《诗经》《尚书》等诸家典籍，一律交郡守等处焚毁；对大批指责非议当时制度与法律政策的儒士大加杀戮，严厉打击一

---

〔1〕参见朱勇主编：《中国法律史》，中国政法大学出版社2021年版，第68页。

切有损于国家法令威信的思想和言论；严禁人民谈论诗书，以古非今。历史上的"焚书坑儒"即肇端于此。对于法家韩非及其"以法为教"的思想，秦始皇则给予了高度评价，称"寡人得见此人与之游，死无憾矣！"秦朝文化思想领域的"独尊法家"政策，使百家争鸣的局面就此完结。这是当时政治上的一种必要举措，也是对文化的一次最严重的摧残。它毁灭了先秦以来大量的文献典籍，也结束了自春秋以来自由思索的蓬勃精神。

图 5-2 陕西靖边：战国秦长城遗址

尽管如此，秦朝法律在中国法律史上依然占有非常重要的地位。秦朝是中国历史上第一个创立全国统一的君主专制的中央集权法律制度的王朝，制定并执行了全国统一的法律、法令、规章、制度。它对全国统一局面的形成和巩固、社会秩序的建立与稳定、经济基础的巩固与发展、生产的发展与社会进步，都起到了积极作用。然而，秦王朝专任刑法，把专制的政治、经济、文化统治推向了极端。秦代"繁法酷刑"、造成"赭衣塞路，囹圄成市"，使商鞅变法以来所形成的法律秩序遭到严重破坏，从而激化了矛盾，加速了秦王朝的崩溃。[1]

〔1〕 参见朱勇主编：《中国法律史》，中国政法大学出版社 2021 年版，第 68~90 页。

◆ 生词表

序号	生词	词性	汉语拼音	英文解释
1	偏僻	*adj.*	piān pì	remote，secluded
2	地处	*v.*	dì chǔ	locate
3	上层建筑	*n.*	shàng céng jiàn zhù	superstructure
4	统治地位	*n.*	tǒng zhì dì wèi	position of rule
5	挟书律	*proper n.*	Xié shū Lǜ	law against private possession of books
6	郡守	*n.*	jùn shǒu	prefect
7	儒士	*n.*	rú shì	Confucianism scholar
8	以古非今	*idm.*	yǐ gǔ fēi jīn	criticize the present by praising the past
9	寡人	*n.*	guǎ rén	I（self-reference by ancient kings）
10	独尊法家	*phr.*	dú zūn fǎ jiā	exclusively honor the Legalist school
11	赭衣塞路	*idm.*	zhě yī sè lù	people in prison garb fill the roads
12	囹圄成市	*idm.*	líng yǔ chéng shì	prisons as crowded as markets
13	制度	*n.*	zhì dù	system，institution
14	经济基础	*n.*	jīng jì jī chǔ	economic base
15	繁法酷刑	*phr.*	fán fǎ kù xíng	overly harsh laws and cruel punishments
16	法家	*proper n.*	Fǎ jiā	Legalism，school of thought in Chinese philosophy
17	崩溃	*v.*	bēng kuì	collapse

重 点汉字【令】

甲骨文和金文中的"令"字由"亼"和"卪"组成。"亼"象征倒置的

"口","卪"象征跪坐的人形。整个字表达了张口（人）向跪坐之下的人（卪）发号施令的场景，本义是命令。古时"令"和"命"原为一个字，后来分化为两个字。

图5-3 "令"字篆刻（王琦 刻）

在甲骨文中，"令"作为动词，表示命令。金文中的"令"也作为动词，表示命令。此外，金文中有"天令"一词，相当于传世典籍中的"天命"，如《录伯（冬戈）簋》的铭文中所载："惠弘天令（命）"，其中"天令"指仁慧、宽大的天命。因为生命是由天所赐，所以"令"从赐予引申到生命、寿命的意思，如《颂鼎》铭文中所载："通彔（禄）、永令（命）"，表示完整的福荫、长久的寿命。另外，在金文中"令"可以作为"铃"的意思，如《成周铃》铭文："王成周令（铃）"。

在秦简中，"令"也用作其本义，即命令，如《睡虎地秦简·秦律十八种》所载："其叚（假）公，叚（假）而有死亡者，亦令其徒、舍人任其叚（假）。"整句意思是，如果有人借用官方的物品，而借用者死亡了，应命令服役的徒众或其舍人负责。此外，"令"还可以用作官名，如《睡虎地秦简·封诊式》："即令令史某齿牛，牛六岁矣"，意指立即命令令史某检查牛的牙齿，牛已经六岁了。

在古籍中，"令"从命令引申出"使、让"的意思，如《程氏家塾读书分年日程》："令，使也"，《战国策·赵策一》："故贵为列侯者，不令在相位。"此外，"令"还有美好的意思，《尔雅·释诂》："令，善也。"《诗·大雅·卷阿》："如圭如璋，令闻令望"，东汉郑玄注解为："令，善也。"

 汉字拓展

序号	词汇	汉语拼音	英文解释	例句
1	命令	mìng lìng	order，command	军队根据指挥官的命令开始行动。
2	令牌	lìng pái	token，emblem	他向守门人展示了进入的令牌。
3	令箭	lìng jiàn	token of military authority	古代将领常用令箭下达紧急军令。
4	指令	zhǐ lìng	directive，instruction	他遵循计算机程序的指令进行操作。
5	节令	jié lìng	season，time of year	春天是播种的节令。
6	县令	xiàn lìng	county magistrate（in ancient China）	他被任命为这个县的县令。
7	如梦令	rú mèng lìng	a type of classical Chinese poem	唐代诗人常以"如梦令"抒发哀愁。
8	令堂	lìng táng	respectful term for other's mother	令堂是位和蔼可亲的女士。
9	令尊	lìng zūn	respectful term for other's father	令尊真是一位伟大的学者！

文 化知识【"书同文 车同轨"】

　　"书同文，车同轨"是秦始皇在统一六国后实施的一项重要政治措施，主要包括两个方面：统一全国的文字和统一车轮的轨距。这些措施是秦始皇加强中央集权和推动国家整体统一的关键步骤。

　　"书同文"指的是统一全国的文字。在秦始皇之前，中国各地的文字存在较大差异，各国使用各自的文字系统，这给交流与管理带来了很大的不便。秦始皇统一六国后，为了加强中央集权和文化统一，推行了统一的小篆文字。这一措施有效地加强了国家的统一性，也促进了文化和经济的交流。

图 5-4　陕西历史博物馆：秦·铜车马（复制品）

"车同轨"则是指统一全国车辆的轨距。古代中国各地的车轮轨距不同，这在交通和军事上造成了很大的不便。秦始皇下令统一轨距，使得车辆能够在全国范围内的道路上通行无阻，特别是对于军事行动和物资运输带来了巨大的便利。统一轨距也标志着交通规则的统一，为后续的道路建设和维护提供了基础。

这两项措施在秦始皇的中央集权体系中扮演了非常重要的角色。通过文字的统一，秦朝能够更加高效地进行法令的发布和实施，增强了政府的行政效率；而通过统一轨距，加强了国内的物流和人员流动，使得秦朝的军事和经济控制能力得到了加强。

"书同文，车同轨"的实施，不仅加快了中国的政治和文化整合，也为中国后世的统一提供了持久影响。这种统一标准的理念，在一定程度上预示了现代国家对标准化的追求，其对中国乃至世界文化的整体发展产生了深远的影响。

法 治文物【八斤铜权】

中国政法大学法律古籍整理研究所

图 5-5　秦·八斤铜权[1]

经 典阅读

《韩非子·十过》：十过：一曰行小忠，则大忠之贼也。二曰顾小利，则大利之残也。三曰行僻自用，无礼诸侯，则亡身之至也。四曰不务听治而好五音，则穷身之事也。五曰贪愎喜利，则灭国杀身之本也。六曰耽于女乐，不顾国政，则亡国之祸也。七曰离内远游而忽于谏士，则危身之道

---

〔1〕秦铜权是秦代青铜器，铸于秦代（公元前 221 年—前 207 年），收藏于中国国家博物馆。铜质，高 5.5 厘米，底径 9.8 厘米，重 2063.5 克。权身刻 12 行 40 字，内容为秦始皇二十六年（公元前 221 年）统一度量衡的诏书，并铸阳文"八斤"二字。按自铭计算，每斤约合 257.925 克。参见《秦·八斤铜权、诏书权》，载中国政法大学中华法制文明虚拟博物馆，https://flgj.cupl.edu.cn/info/1072/2220.htm，最后访问日期：2024 年 9 月 23 日。

也。八曰过而不听于忠臣，而独行其意，则灭高名，为人笑之始也。九曰内不量力，外恃诸侯，则削国之患也。十曰国小无礼，不用谏臣，则绝世之势也。

 参考译文

《韩非子·十过》中列举了一个统治者或国家可能会犯的十大错误：

1. 过分实行小忠诚会成为大忠诚的贼害。意思是过于注重对个人的忠诚，可能会损害到大局上的忠诚。

2. 过分关注小利益会破坏大利益。意味着小利的追求可能会牺牲更大的利益。

3. 行为偏僻自用，不礼遇诸侯，则可能导致身败名裂。指的是行为乖张、自行其是，不尊重其他领导者，会导致严重的后果。

4. 不专注于治理国家，而沉迷于音乐，将导致个人和国家走上末路。说明不务正业，沉溺于娱乐，将耗尽国家和个人资源。

5. 贪婪且固执，喜欢利益，则可能导致国家灭亡和个人身败。表明贪欲和利益的追求是国家和个人灾难的根源。

6. 沉溺于女色和歌舞，不关心国家政务，将是国家灭亡的祸根。强调放纵私欲，忽视国家大事将导致灾难。

7. 疏远内政，远游不听忠臣的劝谏，是危及自身安全的行为。指出领导者如果忽视内部事务，不听从忠诚的建议，将面临危险。

8. 犯错而不听忠臣的劝告，只按自己的意愿行事，将是毁掉好名声和成为众人笑柄的开端。意味着固执己见，不接受忠诚建议将导致声誉受损。

9. 国内不评估自身的力量，国外过分依赖诸侯，将削弱国家。说明过分依赖外部力量而忽视内部发展是危险的。

10. 小国不遵守礼节，不采纳忠臣的建议，将是断绝国家未来的行为。强调即使是小国也应该遵守礼节和重视忠臣的意见，否则将没有未来。

Han Feizi: Ten Faults: ten major mistakes that a ruler or a state might commit are listed:

1. Excessive adherence to minor loyalties can become the enemy of greater loyalty. This means that focusing too much on personal affairs of loyalty may harm overarching fidelity.

2. Overemphasis on minor benefits can destroy major interests. This suggests that pursuing minor gains might sacrifice greater benefits.

3. Engaging in eccentric and self-serving behaviors, and failing to honor other leaders, can lead to ruin and disgrace. This refers to acting bizarrely and independently, disrespecting other leaders, which can lead to severe consequences.

4. Not focusing on governing the country but indulging in music will lead to dead end for both the individual and the nation. This illustrates that neglecting one's duties and indulging in entertainment will deplete both personal and national resources.

5. Being greedy and obstinate with a love for profit can lead to the destruction of the nation and personal downfall. This indicates that the pursuit of greed and benefits is the root of disasters for both the nation and individuals.

6. Indulging in pleasures and music, ignoring national affairs, will be the calamity that leads to the nation's demise. This emphasizes that indulging personal desires while neglecting major state affairs will lead to disaster.

7. Alienating domestic affairs and traveling far without heeding the advice of loyal ministers is a practice that jeopardizes personal safety. This points out that if leaders neglect internal matters and ignore the advice of loyal counselors, they will face danger.

8. Making mistakes and not listening to the counsel of loyal ministers, acting solely according to one's own wishes, marks the beginning of ruining one's reputation and becoming a laughingstock. This means being stubborn and not accepting loyal advice will damage one's reputation.

9. Not assessing one's own strength domestically but overly relying on foreign

lords weaken the state. This explains that excessive dependence on external forces while neglecting internal development is perilous.

10. A small country that does not adhere to protocol and fails to heed the advice of loyal ministers will cut off its future. This emphasizes that even small states should follow protocol and value the opinions of loyal ministers; otherwise, they have no future.

课后练习

1. 选择题：下列哪位历史人物不是以法家思想主导其变法活动的？

A. 商鞅

B. 李悝

C. 申不害

D. 孔子

2. 判断题：秦始皇曾高度评价韩非，并认为能与之交往是一件无憾事情。

3. 填空题：秦始皇为了加强法家思想的影响力，颁布了＿＿＿＿＿＿律，并采取了极端手段来＿＿＿＿＿＿诸子百家的思想。

4. 简答题：描述法家思想如何影响了秦朝的法律制度及其政治、经济、文化方面的统治。

5. 讨论题：探讨秦朝实施法家理论中的"繁法酷刑"对其政治稳定和最终崩溃的影响，并分析这一政策的长期后果。

课文参考翻译

During the Spring and Autumn Period and Warring States Periods, Legalism had the most significant impact on social transformation. Li Kui implemented reforms in Wei, Shen Buhai in Han, and Wu Qi in Chu, all predominantly guided by Legalism philosophy. Located in a remote area and less influenced by Central Plains culture, Qin provided a social foundation for the dissemination of Legalism ideas.

Since Shang Yang's reforms, Legalism political theory and legal thought have played an important guiding role in the political and legal development of Qin. The success of Shang Yang's reforms and the rapid prosperity of Qin further solidified the position of Legalism theory within the upper echelons of Qin. Both before and after unification, the Legalism advocacy of "rule of law" and the strategy of harsh penalties guided Qin rulers. Over a long period of political practice, Qin rulers applied Legalism theory to real politics, forming a series of guiding principles for legal construction.

After the unification of China, the Qin rulers continued to implement Legalism ideas, suppressing the development and dissemination of various schools of thought among the people using extreme measures. Emperor Qin Shihuang issued the "Law on Holding Books," ordering that, except for the "Annals of Qin" produced by official historians and books on medicine, divination, and agriculture, all historical records from other states and privately held classics like the *The Book of Songs* and *The Book of Documents* should be surrendered to local authorities for burning. He also massacred many scholars who criticized the current system and legal policies, severely cracking down on any thoughts and speeches that undermined the authority of national laws; discussing poetry and the classics was strictly forbidden. The historical episode of "Burning of Books and Burying of Confucianism Scholars" began from this. Emperor Qin Shihuang highly praised Han Fei's Legalism idea of "using law as instruction," proclaiming, "If I could meet this man and converse with him, I would die without regrets!" The policy of "sole reverence for Legalism" during the Qin dynasty ended the contention of a hundred schools of thought. This was a necessary political measure at the time but also a severe devastation to culture. It destroyed a vast amount of literature and documents since the pre-Qin period and ended the vibrant spirit of free thought that had flourished since the Spring and Autumn Period.

Despite this, Qin's legal system still holds a very important place in the history of Chinese law. The Qin dynasty was the first in Chinese history to establish a centralized legal system under an autocratic monarchy, enacting and enforcing unified laws, decrees, regulations, and systems nationwide. It played a positive role in forming and consolidating national unity, establishing and stabilizing social order, strengthening the economic foundation, and promoting the development of production and social progress. However, Qin's excessive laws and severe punishments, pushing the autocratic rule of politics, economy, and culture to the extreme, severely damaged the legal order established since Shang Yang's reforms, intensifying conflicts and accelerating the collapse of the Qin dynasty.

汉朝时期的法律（一）

课 前准备

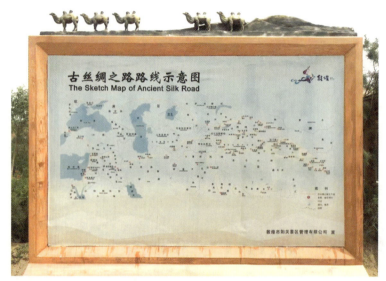

图 6-1　甘肃敦煌阳关景区：古丝绸之路路线示意图

　　汉朝（公元前 202 年—公元 220 年），是中国继秦朝之后的大一统王朝，分为西汉、东汉两个时期，一共有 29 个皇帝。

　　秦末农民起义，刘邦推翻秦后被封为汉王。楚汉争霸，刘邦战胜项羽并称帝建立汉朝，定都长安（今西安），史称西汉。汉文帝、汉景帝看到了秦朝灭亡的教训，推行休养生息的国策。汉武帝即位后，"罢黜百家，独尊儒术"、加强中央集权，派张骞出使西域，沟通中原与西域各国的联系，开辟丝绸之路。著名的佛教艺术圣地——敦煌——就是在汉朝时期成为"丝绸之路"上的咽喉重镇。汉宣帝时期，西汉的国力达到极盛，设立西域都护府，将西域纳入版图。

　　公元 25 年刘秀重建汉朝，定都洛阳，史称东汉。刘秀统一天下后息兵养民。军事上迫使匈奴西迁，派班超经营西域，丝绸之路延伸至欧洲。公元 100 年罗马帝国遣使来朝，东汉国力趋于极盛。

公元 190 年，军阀四起，天下大乱。公元 220 年曹丕篡汉，定都洛阳，史称曹魏，汉朝灭亡。

汉朝是当时世界上最先进的文明及强大的帝国。两汉极盛时，东并朝鲜、南包越南、西逾葱岭、北达蒙古。华夏族自汉朝以后逐渐被称为汉族，文字被称为"汉字"。

汉朝的法律，和秦朝相比，发生了巨变。主要经历两个阶段：第一个阶段，从汉朝建立之初，到汉武帝亲政，以"黄老"学说为主，辅之以"儒、法"；在法制上，主要表现为"与民休息"。第二个阶段自汉武帝"罢黜百家独尊儒术"开始，法律开始逐渐以儒为主，礼法并用。而中国封建社会的法制，也开始了儒家化的过程。

The Han Dynasty (202 BC-AD 220) was a grand unified dynasty in China following the Qin Dynasty, divided into the Western and Eastern Han periods, with a total of 29 emperors.

At the end of the Qin Dynasty, amidst peasant uprisings, Liu Bang overthrew the Qin and was crowned King of Han. After defeating Xiang Yu in the Chu-Han contention, Liu Bang declared himself emperor and founded the Han Dynasty, establishing the capital at Chang'an (present-day Xi'an), known historically as the Western Han. Emperors Wen and Jing of Han learned from the downfall of the Qin and implemented policies of rest and recuperation. Emperor Wu, after coming to power, "dismissed all other schools of thought to promote only Confucianism," strengthened central authority, and sent Zhang Qian as an envoy to the Western Regions to establish connections between the Central Plains and the Western Regions, thus opening up the Silk Road. The famous Buddhist art site—Dunhuang—became a strategic pass on the Silk Road during the Han Dynasty. Under Emperor Xuan of Han, the Western Han reached its zenith, establishing the Protectorate of the Western Regions and incorporating them into its territory.

In AD 25, Liu Xiu restored the Han Dynasty, setting the capital at Luoyang, historically known as the Eastern Han. After unifying China, Liu Xiu focused on rebuilding and recuperating. Militarily, he forced the Xiongnu to migrate westward, sent Ban Chao to manage the Western Regions, and extended the Silk Road to Europe. By AD 100, the Roman Empire sent emissaries to the court, marking the peak of the Eastern Han's power.

By AD 190, warlords rose up, plunging the realm into chaos. In AD 220, Cao Pi usurped the Han, establishing his capital at Luoyang and marking the rise of Cao Wei, leading to the fall of the Han Dynasty.

The Han Dynasty was the most advanced civilization and powerful empire in the world at that time. At its height, it expanded east to Korea, south to Vietnam, west beyond the Congling Mountains, and north to Mongolia. From the Han Dynasty onwards, the Huaxia people gradually came to be known as the Han ethnic group, and their script as "Han characters."

The legal system of the Han Dynasty underwent significant changes compared to the Qin Dynasty, primarily in two stages: Initially, from the establishment of the Han to Emperor Wu's personal rule, the predominant philosophy was Huang-Lao, supplemented by Confucian and Legalist principles, with laws focusing on "resting with the people." From Emperor Wu's promotion of Confucianism, law gradually leaned towards Confucian ideals, integrating rituals and laws. This marked the beginning of the Confucianization of legal systems in Chinese feudal society.

 生词表

序号	生词	词性	汉语拼音	英文解释
1	大一统	*n.*	dà yī tǒng	grand unification
2	皇帝	*n.*	huáng dì	emperor
3	楚汉争霸	*phr.*	Chǔ Hàn zhēng bà	Chu-Han contention
4	休养生息	*phr.*	xiū yǎng shēng xī	recuperate and multiply

续表

序号	生词	词性	汉语拼音	英文解释
5	罢黜百家	*phr.*	bà chù bǎi jiā	dismiss all other schools of thought
6	独尊儒术	*phr.*	dú zūn rú shù	solely honor Confucianism
7	丝绸之路	*proper n.*	Sī chóu zhī lù	Silk Road
8	都护府	*n.*	dū hù fǔ	Protectorate
9	匈奴	*proper n.*	Xiōng nú	Xiongnu, an ancient nomadic tribe

导读

　　西汉和东汉前后存续一共 400 余年，是中国历史上第一个盛世，不仅继承并发扬了秦朝开创的中央集权的皇帝政治法律制度，也纠正了秦王朝严刑峻法的弊端。两汉时期，传统法律文化自汉初便开始了儒家化的过程，其间从思想到体制，虽然几经反复，但法律儒家化的进程却始终如一。[1]

课文

　　秦朝的法律以其严苛和残酷闻名，在秦始皇死后，秦朝的局势变得动荡不安。秦始皇的儿子胡亥继位后，由于他的无能和轻信奸臣赵高，导致许多忠诚的大臣被错误地处决。胡亥的统治充满了混乱和不公，加之秦朝法律的苛刻，使得人民生活困苦，因此各地爆发了反抗秦朝的起义。

　　在这一系列反抗中，两位名将刘邦和项羽成为起义军的关键人物。他们原本是楚怀王军队中的将领。楚怀王为了激励他们，提出了一个挑战：谁能率先进入关中，谁就能称王。这一激励极大地刺激了刘邦和项羽的野心，他们各自率领军队踏上了征程。

---

　　[1]　参见朱勇主编：《中国法律史》，中国政法大学出版社 2021 年版，第 91 页。

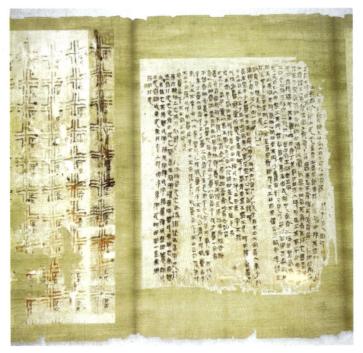

图 6-2　湖南博物院：西汉·帛书《刑德》甲本

　　刘邦的军队在途中连战连胜，最终顺利进入了关中的咸阳城。但是，取得了胜利后，刘邦开始沉迷于奢华的生活，每天与美酒和美女为伍，忘记了初心和使命。幸好，他的谋士张良及时出现，提醒并劝导他回归正途。刘邦这才醒悟，召集了他的部下进行会议，约法三章：凡杀人者处死，伤人和偷盗者抵罪，其他秦朝的苛刻法律全部废除。[1]这些政策一经宣布，立即赢得了官员和百姓的广泛支持，使刘邦迅速获得了民心。

　　古语有云："得民心者得天下。"刘邦的智慧和政策改革为他赢得了人民的广泛支持，这成为他最终取得胜利的关键。在与项羽的长期斗争后，刘邦最终战胜了项羽，建立了汉朝，并被尊称为汉高祖。他的统治标志着中国历史上一个新时代的开始。汉高祖刘邦的故事至今仍被视为智慧和勇气的象征，他的统治不仅结束了秦朝的暴政，也为后世树立了以民为本的治国典范。

―――――――――――――

　　〔1〕原文参考"约法三章"，载（汉）司马迁所著《史记·高祖本纪》："父老苦秦苛法久矣……与父老约法三章耳：杀人者死，伤人及盗抵罪，余悉除去秦法。"

生词表

序号	生词	词性	汉语拼音	英文解释
1	严苛	*adj.*	yán kē	harsh，severe
2	残酷	*adj.*	cán kù	cruel
3	动荡不安	*adj.*	dòng dàng bù ān	unstable，turbulent
4	奸臣	*n.*	jiān chén	treacherous official
5	错误地	*adv.*	cuò wù de	erroneously
6	混乱	*n.*	hùn luàn	chaos
7	苛刻	*adj.*	kē kè	harsh，stringent
8	疾苦	*n.*	jí kǔ	suffering，hardship
9	起义军	*n.*	qǐ yì jūn	rebel army
10	挑战	*n.*	tiǎo zhàn	challenge
11	沉迷	*v.*	chén mí	indulge
12	初心	*n.*	chū xīn	original intention，aspiration
13	使命	*n.*	shǐ mìng	mission
14	谋士	*n.*	móu shì	strategist，counselor
15	政策改革	*phr.*	zhèng cè gǎi gé	policy reform
16	治国	*phr.*	zhì guó	govern a country
17	典范	*n.*	diǎn fàn	model，example

重 点汉字【罚】

　　"罚"始见于西周金文。"罚"的结构从现代汉字的构字要素来看，由"罒"（网）、"讠"（言）和"刂"（刀）组合而成。"罚"字在小篆以前，右旁从"刀"，左旁从"罒"（网）和"讠"（言），多为左右结构。隶变后，刀旁（汉代刀旁或讹为寸旁）移至网（后世位于字形上部者，多写为"罒"）下，字形遂变为上下结构，而为楷书所本。银雀山汉简文字或省去"网"而作从言从刀。现代汉字简化时则将"言"简化为"讠"，简作"罚"。许慎《说文解字》这样说解"罪"字：罚是轻微的犯法行为。由刀、由詈会意。没有用刀对人有所伤害，只拿着刀骂人，就应该处罚。许慎认为"罚"由"刀"和表示骂的"詈"会意，意思是小的罪。

图 6-3 "罚"字篆刻（王琦 刻）

 ## 汉字拓展

序号	词汇	汉语拼音	英文解释	例句
1	罚款	fá kuǎn	fine	他因违章停车被罚款。
2	处罚	chǔ fá	punishment	违反规则的员工将受到处罚。
3	罚单	fá dān	ticket，fine slip	他收到了一张超速驾驶的罚单。
4	罚金	fá jīn	monetary penalty	未按时还书将被收取罚金。
5	罚球	fá qiú	penalty kick（in sports）	足球比赛中，他成功射入了一个罚球。
6	罚点球	fá diǎn qiú	penalty shot（in football/soccer）	球队获得了一个罚点球的机会。
7	体罚	tǐ fá	corporal punishment	现代教育中已经严格禁止体罚。
8	罚站	fá zhàn	punishment of standing	上课迟到的学生被罚站一小时。

化知识【"更"与"宵禁"】

　　古代的一更就是现在的晚上 7 点到 9 点（戌时），此后 9 点到 11 点为二更（亥时），夜里 11 点到凌晨 1 点为三更（子时三更半夜），凌晨 1 点到 3 点为四更（丑时），凌晨 3 点到 5 点为五更（寅时）。

图 6-4　阳关博物馆："李广骑射"画砖像 （复制品）

　　"宵禁"是指古代禁止百姓夜行的制度，从商周时期就有了宵禁令，直至 1924 年才逐步废除。在古代，只有上元节，也就是元宵节（正月十五），能在外面一整晚。在有宵禁令的朝代，天黑还不回家，就是犯罪，罪名称"犯夜"。

　　关于"宵禁"，《汉书·李广传》中有一个著名的案例：彼时，汉代名将李广被贬为庶人，这天，李广带着一个随从骑马外出，和朋友在郊外饮酒。回到霸陵亭的时候，恰好霸陵尉喝醉了，大声斥责李广，李广的随从回答说："这位是过去的李将军。"霸陵尉回答："就是现在的将军也不许晚上出来，何况是过去的将军！"于是，就让李广直接待在了霸陵亭下。

　　汉朝法律把宵禁令称为"夜禁"，并作出了详细的规定：一更三点暮鼓一敲，禁止出行；想要出门，就要等到五更三点晨钟响了才行。要是二、三、四更还在街上逛的，打四十下，若是在京城街上逛的，就要打五十下。只有因疾病、生育、死丧等事由可以在宵禁期间得到豁免。

此外，每逢朝廷有重大庆典的时候，因需要前一天通夜准备，也会暂时解除或开放宵禁。盛世之际，皇帝会赐宴臣民聚会欢饮，被称为"赐酺"，一般会有三天时间的大吃大喝，不加禁止。

法 治文物【汉·《甘露二年丞相御史书》】

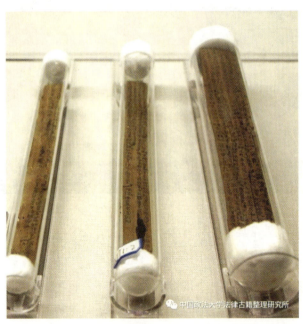

图 6-5　汉·《甘露二年丞相御史书》[1]

---

〔1〕参见《汉·〈甘露二年丞相御史书〉》，载中国政法大学中华法制文明虚拟博物馆，https://flgj.cupl.edu.cn/info/1091/1558.htm，最后访问日期：2024 年 10 月 22 日。

经 典阅读

《春秋繁露·五行之义》天有五行：一曰木，二曰火，三曰土，四曰金，五曰水。木，五行之始也；水，五行之终也；土，五行之中也。此其天次之序也。木生火，火生土，土生金，金生水，水生木，此其父子也。木居左，金居右，火居前，水居后，土居中央，此其父子之序，相受而布。是故木受水，而火受木，土受火，金受土，水受金也。诸授之者，皆其父也；受之者，皆其子也。常因其父以使其子，天之道也。是故木已生而火养之，金已死而水藏之，火乐木而养以阳，水克金而丧以阴，土之事天竭其忠。故五行者，乃孝子忠臣之行也。

五行之为言也，犹五行与？是故以得辞也，圣人知之，故多其爱而少严，厚养生而谨送终，就天之制也。以子而迎成养，如火之乐木也。丧父，如水之克金也。事君，若土之敬天也。可谓有行人矣。

五行之随，各如其序，五行之官，各致其能。是故木居东方而主春气，火居南方而主夏气，金居西方而主秋气，水居北方而主冬气。是故木主生而金主杀，火主暑而水主寒，使人必以其序，官人必以其能，天之数也。土居中央，为之天润。土者，天之股肱也。其德茂美，不可名以一时之事，故五行而四时者。土兼之也。金木水火虽各职，不因土，方不立，若酸咸辛苦之不因甘肥不能成味也。甘者，五味之本也；土者，五行之主也。五行之主土气也，犹五味之有甘肥也，不得不成。是故圣人之行，莫贵于忠，土德之谓也。人官之大者，不名所职，相其是矣。天官之大者，不名所生，土是矣。

◆ 参考译文

五行包括：第一是木，第二是火，第三是土，第四是金，第五是水。木代表五行的开始，水代表五行的结束，土则位于五行的中心。这是自然界中五行的天然顺序。木生火，火生土，土生金，金生水，水又生木，这表明它们之间的父子关系。木位于左边，金位于右边，火位于前面，水位于后面，土位于中央，这是它们作为父子的顺序，相互影响和布局。因此，木得水而生长，火从木中得到生长，土从火中得到生长，金从土中得到生长，水从金中得到生长。给予的是父亲，接受的是儿子。自然界常常是通过父亲来影响儿子，这是天道。因此，木已经生长而火则维持其生长，金已经消亡而水则隐藏其精华，火喜欢木而用阳光来滋养它，水克制金而用阴气为它送终，土对天尽忠。因此，五行是孝顺的儿子和忠诚的臣子的行为典范。

五行的讨论，不就是说五种德行吗？因此，它得名于此，圣人明白这个道理。因此他们更加爱护而少施严厉，厚养生命而谨慎处理死亡，这符合天道的安排。比如子女对父母的养育，就像火对木的喜爱。子女为父母送终，就像水对金的送终。臣下侍奉君王，就像土对天的敬仰。这样便称得上有德行的人。

五行各随其序，五行的官职各尽其能。因此，木主宰东方和春季，火主宰南方和夏季，金主宰西方和秋季，水主宰北方和冬季。木主生长而金主杀戮，火主炎热而水主寒冷，人必须遵循这一顺序，官员必须依据这些能力，这是天的法则。土居中央，使天地得以滋润。土是天的臂膀。它的美德是丰富而美好的，不能仅用一个季节来形容，因此有五行却只有四季，因为土兼管四季。虽然金木水火各有其职责，但如果没有土，它们就不能确定各自方位，就像没有甘甜，则酸、咸、辣、苦就不能形成味道一样。甘甜是五味之本，土是五行之主。五行之中，土气是主导，就像五味中有甘甜那样，不可或缺。因此，圣人行为中最为重要的是忠诚，这是土的美德。人的高官，不以其专有的职务为名，宰相就是这样的。天的高官，不以所专有事务为名，土就是这样的。

The Five Elements include: first, Wood; second, Fire; third, Earth; fourth, Metal; fifth, Water. Wood represents the beginning of the Five Elements, Water represents the end, and Earth is located at the center. This is the natural order of the Five Elements in nature. Wood generates Fire, Fire generates Earth, Earth generates Metal, Metal generates Water, and Water generates Wood, which demonstrates their intergenerational relationships. Wood is placed on the left, Metal on the right, Fire in front, Water behind, and Earth in the center. This is their order as parent and child, influencing and arranging each other. Therefore, Wood thrives with Water, Fire grows from Wood, Earth from Fire, Metal from Earth, and Water from Metal. Those that give are their fathers, and those that receive are their sons. It is a natural law that the father influences the son. Hence, Wood once grown is nourished by Fire, Metal once dead is concealed by Water, Fire enjoys Wood and nourishes it with sunlight, Water overcomes Metal and brings coolness to pay the last respect, Earth loyally serves the heavens. Thus, the Five Elements exemplify filial sons and loyal ministers.

The discussion of the Five Elements seems to be about the Five virtues. Therefore, through such discussions, the sages understood this, thus they cared more and imposed less harshness, nurtured life generously and handled death with caution, aligning with the heavenly order. For instance, children's care for their parents is like Fire's affection for Wood. The loss of a father is like Water seeing Metal out. Serving a sovereign is like Earth venerating the heavens. It can be said that these are virtuous applications.

Each of the Five Elements follows its sequence, and the officials of the Elements perform according to their capabilities. Therefore, Wood governs the East and the spring, Fire governs the South and the summer, Metal governs the West and the autumn, Water governs the North and the winter. Wood is associated with growth and Metal with termination, Fire with heat and Water with cold. People must follow this order, and officials must act according to these abilities, as decreed by the heavens. Earth is located at the center, enriching heaven and earth. Earth is the arm of heaven. Its virtues are abundant and beautiful, not limited to a single season, hence while there are Four Seasons, Earth encompasses all. Although Metal, Wood, Water, and Fire each have their roles, without Earth, they cannot stand alone, just as flavors (sour, saltiness, spiciness, bitterness) cannot form without sweetness. Sweetness is the basis of the five flavors; Earth is the leader of the Five Elements. The dominating force among the Five Elements is the Earth element, just as sweetness is essential among the five flavors. Therefore, the most valuable behavior of the sages is loyalty, which is the virtue of Earth. High officials among people do not define themselves by their exclusive position, the Chancellor is just like that. The greatest officials of heaven are not defined by their proprietary transaction; Earth is just like that.

课 后练习

1. 选择题：秦二世统治失败的主要原因是什么？

A. 经济政策

B. 军事战略

C. 无能和轻信奸臣

D. 外交政策

2. 判断题：刘邦在成为汉高祖前，曾因沉迷奢华而忘记初心，直到张良的提醒才使他回归正途。

3. 填空题：秦二世统治期间，民间疾苦导致_____起义频发，最终导致了_____的崩溃。

4. 简答题：描述刘邦实施的三项政策，并解释它们是如何帮助他赢得民心的。

5. 讨论题：探讨秦末民变的社会背景和刘邦、项羽的军事策略对于秦朝崩溃的影响，以及这些事件如何反映了法家思想在实际政治中的应用和局限性。

课 文参考翻译

The laws of the Qin Dynasty were notorious for their severity and brutality. After the death of Emperor Qin Shihuang, the situation in the Qin Dynasty became increasingly unstable. His son, Huhai, succeeded him, but due to his incompetence and his gullible trust in the treacherous minister Zhao Gao, many loyal ministers were wrongly executed. The rule of Huhai was filled with chaos and injustice, compounded by the harsh Qin laws, which caused great suffering among the populace. As a result, uprisings against the Qin Dynasty erupted across the land.

Among the leaders of these rebellions, two prominent generals, Liu Bang and Xiang Yu, emerged as key figures. They were originally commanders in the army of King Huai of Chu. To motivate them, King Huai declared that whoever could first enter the region of Guanzhong would be granted kingship. This challenge greatly stimulated the ambitions of Liu Bang and Xiang Yu, and they each led their armies on a march towards Guanzhong.

Liu Bang's army achieved successive victories along the way and eventually entered Xianyang, the city of Guanzhong. However, after his victory, Liu Bang became engrossed in a life of luxury, indulging daily in fine wine and beautiful women, forgetting his original purpose and mission. Fortunately, his advisor Zhang Liang appeared in time to remind and counsel him to return to the right path. Awakened by this advice, Liu Bang gathered his subordinates for a meeting and formulated three important policies: Anyone who committed murder would be executed; those who caused injury or theft would be punished; and all other harsh laws of the Qin Dynasty would be abolished. Once these policies were announced, they immediately gained widespread support from both officials and common people, quickly winning the hearts of the populace.

As an ancient saying goes, "He who wins the hearts of the people, wins the world." Liu Bang's wisdom and policy reforms earned him widespread support from the people, which was crucial to his ultimate victory. After a prolonged struggle with Xiang Yu, Liu Bang finally defeated him, establishing the Han Dynasty and being honored as Emperor Gaozu of Han. His reign marked the beginning of a new era in Chinese history. The story of Emperor Gaozu of Han, Liu Bang, remains a symbol of wisdom and courage to this day. His rule not only ended the tyranny of the Qin Dynasty but also set a precedent for a governance model that prioritized the welfare of the people for future generations.

汉朝时期的法律（二）

课 前准备

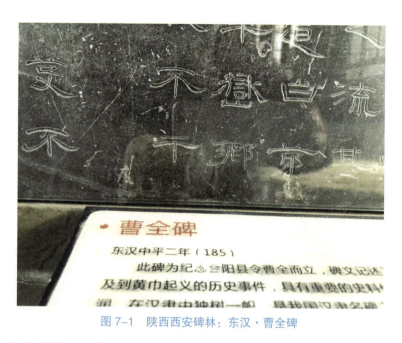

图7-1　陕西西安碑林：东汉·曹全碑

　　两汉相沿的400余年中，中国传统立法也有了长足的进步，无论在立法内容、立法技术以及法律形式等各个方面，比前代都有明显的发展和进步。一般来说，汉代的主要立法集中在汉初高祖、吕后以及文景之世，至中期武帝时立法已较为全面。经过初、中期的全面立法，两汉法律制度的主要内容和风格均已形成，此间所制定的主要法律规范作为祖宗成宪，贯穿整个两汉期间。其中，西汉的主要立法活动如"约法三章"、《九章律》、《傍章律》、《越宫律》、《朝律》等。《朝律》又称为《朝贺律》，是关于朝贺制度的专门法规，与《越宫律》《九章律》《傍章律》一起，合称"汉律六十篇"。光武中兴东汉建立，史载："至天下已定，务用安静，解王莽之繁密，还汉世之轻法。"

　　Over more than 400 years of the Western and Eastern Han dynasties, Chinese traditional legislation has made significant progress in various aspects, including legislative content, technique and legal forms, clearly advancing beyond previous eras. Generally, the main legislative activities of the Han dynasty were concentrated around the era of Emperor Gaozu, Empress Lyv and the Emperors Wen and Jing, with more comprehensive legislation during the reign of Emperor Wu in the mid-period. Through the initial and middle phases, the main content and style of Han legal systems were established. The primary legal norms formulated during this period, known as ancestral constitutions, were upheld throughout the Han dynasty. Key legislative activities in the Western Han included "three-point covenant," the "Nine Chapters Law," "Bangzhang Code," "Yuegong Law," and "Morning Court Law." The "Morning Court Law," also known as "Morning Greetings Law," focused specifically on the court greeting system and, together with the "Yuegong Law," "Nine Chapters Law," and "Bangzhang Code," was collectively referred to as the "Sixty Articles of Han Law." With the restoration of the Eastern Han by Emperor Guangwu, historical records state, "Once the empire was stabilized, efforts focused on maintaining peace, reducing the complexities of Wang Mang's regulations, and reverting to the lighter laws of the Han era."

 生词表

序号	生词	词性	汉语拼音	英文解释
1	相沿	*v.*	xiāng yán	follow，be in line with
2	长足	*adj.*	cháng zú	rapid，substantial
3	立法	*v.*	lì fǎ	legislate
4	高祖	*n.*	gāo zǔ	high ancestor，title for an emperor
5	文景之世	*phr.*	wén jǐng zhī shì	the era of Emperors Wen and Jing of Han dynasty
6	全面	*adj.*	quán miàn	comprehensive

续表

序号	生词	词性	汉语拼音	英文解释
7	祖宗	*n.*	zǔ zōng	ancestor
8	成宪	*n.*	chéng xiàn	established legal system
9	约法三章	*idm.*	yuē fǎ sān zhāng	three-point covenant
10	九章律	*proper n.*	Jiǔ zhāng Lǜ	the main body of Han Law
11	傍章律	*proper n.*	Bàng zhāng Lǜ	the law about etiquette
12	越宫律	*proper n.*	Yuè gōng Lǜ	the law about the palace guards
13	朝律	*proper n.*	Cháo Lǜ	the law about the minister congratulate the emperor
14	朝贺律	*proper n.*	Cháo hè Lǜ	anotner name for "Morning Court Law"
15	朝贺	*n.*	cháo hè	morning greeting（to the emperor）
16	光武中兴	*proper n.*	Guāng wǔ Zhōng xīng	restoration of Eastern Han by Emperor Guangwu
17	繁密	*adj.*	fán mì	complex，intricate
18	轻法	*n.*	qīng fǎ	lenient law

    作为中国古代传统法律制度确立的基本标志的汉律，其特点在于开始把儒家所倡导的礼、义规范纳入法律法令之中，把儒家的经典条文化和法律化，把维护"亲亲""尊尊"为核心的社会政治等级秩序作为自己的首要任务。客观上，传统法律制度的一些基本原则和制度如"亲亲相隐"、上请等，都已经初步形成，十恶八议制度也开始萌芽。特别是汉代中期以后，儒家思想在立法和司法中的地位逐步确立，对中国传统法律特别是刑事立法制度的发展，产生了极为深远的影响。[1]

---

〔1〕 参见朱勇主编：《中国法律史》，中国政法大学出版社 2021 年版，第 101 页。

哀公问孔子："大礼是什么样的？为何君子如此推崇礼呢？"孔子回答："我孔丘只是一个普通的百姓，怎么能了解礼呢？"哀公说："不！我想听你的看法！"孔子回答说："我听说过：人们赖以生活的事物中，礼是最重要的。没有礼，就无法规范祭祀天地神灵的事宜；没有礼，就无法区分君臣、上下、长幼的位置；没有礼，就无法区别男女、父子、兄弟的亲密关系，以及姻亲、朋友之间交情的厚薄。因此，君子把礼看得十分重要。然后，他们尽其所能教育百姓，使他们不失时节地按礼行事。事情有成效后，再讲究什么样的人使用什么样的宫室雕刻、用什么样的祭器、穿什么样的礼服，以区别尊卑上下等级的不同，等等。百姓顺从之后，再给百姓制定服丧的期限，使他们准备好祭祀的器皿，设置祭品，修缮宗庙，按季节举行庄重的祭祀，排序宗族关系。然后君子在自己的居所安居，简化衣服，使宫室简朴、车辆无华丽装饰、器物无复杂雕刻、饮食无过多调味，以此与民共享利益。古代君子行礼的方式就是这样。"

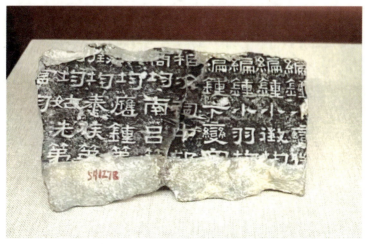

图 7-2　河南博物院：东汉·熹平石经《乐经》残石

原文参考

哀公问于孔子曰："大礼何如？君子之言礼，何其尊也？"孔子曰："丘也小人，何足以知礼？"君曰："否！吾子言之也！"孔子曰："丘闻之也：民之所由生，礼为大。非礼无以节事天地之神明也，非礼无以辨君臣上下长幼之位也，非礼无以别男女父子兄弟之亲、昏姻、疏数之交也，君子以此之为尊敬然。然后以其所能教百姓，不废其会节。有成事，然后治其雕镂文章黼黻以嗣。其顺之，然后言其丧算，备其鼎俎，设其豕腊，修其宗庙，岁时以敬祭祀，以序宗族，则安其居处，丑其衣服，卑其宫室，车不雕几，器不刻镂，食不贰味，以与民同利，昔之君子之行礼者如此。"

 生词表

序号	生词	词性	汉语拼音	英文解释
1	推崇	v.	tuī chóng	highly respect or advocate
2	祭祀	v.	jì sì	offer sacrifices to gods
3	君臣	phr.	jūn chén	ruler and minister
4	上下	phr.	shàng xià	senior and junior
5	长幼	phr.	zhǎng yòu	elders and youngsters
6	亲密关系	n.	qīn mì guān xì	close relationship
7	姻亲	n.	yīn qīn	relation by marriage
8	服丧	phr.	fú sāng	be in mourning
9	器皿	n.	qì mǐn	utensils，vessels
10	庄重	adj.	zhuāng zhòng	solemn，dignified
11	简化	v.	jiǎn huà	simplify
12	宫室	n.	gōng shì	palace rooms
13	华丽	adj.	huá lì	gorgeous，splendid
14	装饰	n.	zhuāng shì	decoration

重 点汉字【约】

"约"原义是用绳捆绑、缠束。其甲骨文是会意字，像人将绳子缠绕在草木上，使其正直，因此有"约束"的含义，"约"的金文是由"糸/系/束"和刀组成；篆文将金文字形中的偏旁再变形，将金文字形中的"刀"写成"勺"；隶化后的楷书将篆文字形中的"系"写成"糹"，将篆文字形中的"刀"写成"勺"，字形即变为"约"，跳出古文字行列。之后，1986年新版简化字总表中的第二表简化偏旁中规定"糹"简化为"纟"，因此，"約"类推简化为今天的"约"。

图 7-3 "约"字篆刻（王琦 刻）

 汉字拓展

序号	词汇	汉语拼音	英文解释	例句
1	预约	yù yuē	make an appointment	我已经预约了明天的医生门诊。
2	约定	yuē dìng	agree，arrange	他们约定下周一见面。
3	约会	yuē huì	date，appointment	他们周末计划去公园约会。
4	约束	yuē shù	restraint，restriction	他遵守了合同的约束条款。

续表

序号	词汇	汉语拼音	英文解释	例句
5	约稿	yuē gǎo	commission（for writing）	杂志社向她发出了约稿的邀请。
6	要约	yào yuē	offer（in contract law）	他向对方提出了一个正式的要约。
7	邀约	yāo yuē	invitation	他收到了参加会议的邀约。
8	节约	jié yuē	save，economize	我们应该节约用水。
9	大约	dà yuē	approximately，about	这项工程大约需要两个月的时间。
10	约谈	yuē tán	talk，discuss	经理约谈了员工，讨论其工作表现。
11	约定俗成	yuē dìng sú chéng	conventionally agreed upon	这个习惯是约定俗成的，大家都这么做。

文 化知识【"投笔从戎"】

图 7-4　河南博物院：东汉·胡汉战争汉画像砖

东汉初期，出现了一位名叫班超的传奇英雄，他是《汉书》作者班固的兄弟，出生于平陵（今陕西省咸阳市西北）。班超自幼刻苦耐劳，勤于学习。因家境贫寒，他青年时经常为官府抄写文件，同时也为私人抄写书籍以赚取微薄的收入，以此来供养整个家庭。

当时，匈奴不断侵扰汉朝边境，班超对此深感愤慨。同时，他也意识到东汉与西域各国的交流已经中断超过五十年。一次，他在抄写文件时，感到无比沮丧，突然站起身来，猛地扔掉手中的笔，慷慨激昂地说道："大丈夫应当立功于异域，如傅介子、张骞那样，怎能一直沉浸于文字工作中呢？"这番言论后被记载于《后汉书·班超传》。

傅介子和张骞都是早期通过出使西域为汉朝立下功勋的人物。傅介子在汉昭帝时期曾出使大宛国和楼兰、龟兹等地。而张骞更早地在汉武帝时期出使月氏，并在被匈奴扣留十多年后逃回中原，之后还曾前往乌孙和其他几个西域国家，促使这些地区与汉朝建立友好关系。到了东汉班超所在的时代，汉朝与西域的联系已然断绝。班超因此萌生了恢复这些联系的壮志。

班超决定放弃文职，加入军队成为一名军官。在哈密地区，他成功地打击了匈奴并取得了胜利。后来，他提出重启与西域的联系，得到东汉朝廷的批准，并被任命为副使，与正使郭恂一起出使西域。这一任务持续了31年，在此期间，班超代表汉王朝与超过五十个国家建立了外交关系。当他71岁高龄归国时，已经完成了年轻时的宏愿。

班超的这段经历被称为"投笔从戎"，这个成语后来用来形容放弃文职转而从军的人。

法 治文物【"獬豸"博物馆（五）】

图 7-5　汉代画像石上的独角兽[1]

---

〔1〕 参见李雪梅：《谜一样的独角兽（一）》，载《中国法律评论》2021 年第 2 期。

典阅读

《汉乐府·陌上桑》

日出东南隅，照我秦氏楼。秦氏有好女，自名为罗敷。罗敷喜蚕桑，采桑城南隅。青丝为笼系，桂枝为笼钩。头上倭堕髻，耳中明月珠。缃绮为下裙，紫绮为上襦。行者见罗敷，下担捋髭须。少年见罗敷，脱帽着帩头。耕者忘其犁，锄者忘其锄。来归相怨怒，但坐观罗敷。

使君从南来，五马立踟蹰。使君遣吏往，问是谁家姝？"秦氏有好女，自名为罗敷。""罗敷年几何？""二十尚不足，十五颇有余。"使君谢罗敷："宁可共载不？"

罗敷前置辞："使君一何愚！使君自有妇，罗敷自有夫。"

"东方千余骑，夫婿居上头。何用识夫婿？白马从骊驹；青丝系马尾，黄金络马头；腰中鹿卢剑，可值千万余。十五府小吏，二十朝大夫，三十侍中郎，四十专城居。为人洁白皙，鬑鬑颇有须。盈盈公府步，冉冉府中趋。坐中数千人，皆言夫婿殊。"

◆ 参考译文

太阳从东南方升起，照到我们秦家的小楼。秦家有位美丽的女儿，自家起名叫做罗敷。罗敷善于养蚕采桑，（有一天在）城南边采桑。她用青丝做篮子上的络绳，用桂树枝做篮子上的提柄。罗敷头上梳着堕马髻，耳朵上戴着宝珠做的耳环；浅黄色有花纹的丝绸做成下裙，紫色的绫子做成上身短袄。走路的人看见罗敷，放下担子捋着胡子（注视她）。看见罗敷，年轻人禁不住脱帽重整头巾，耕地的人忘记了自己在犁地，锄地的人忘记了自己在锄地；回来后相互埋怨（未完成农活），只顾着仔细看了罗敷的美貌。

太守乘车从南边来到这，拉车的五匹马停下来徘徊不前。太守派遣小吏过去，问：这是谁家美丽的女子。答：秦家有位美丽的女儿，叫做罗敷。"罗敷多少岁了？""还不到二十岁，但已经过了十五了。"太守问罗敷："愿意与我一起乘车吗？"

罗敷上前回话："太守你怎么这样愚蠢！太守你已经有妻子了，罗敷我也已经有丈夫了！"

"（我的丈夫当官）在东方，随从人马一千多，他排列在最前头。怎么识别我丈夫呢？骑白马后面跟随小黑马的那个大官就是，用青丝拴着马尾，那马头上戴着金黄色的笼头；腰中佩着鹿卢剑，宝剑价值千万。他十五岁在太守府做小吏，二十岁在朝廷里做大夫，三十岁做皇上的侍中郎，四十岁成为一城之主。他皮肤洁白，有一些胡子；他轻缓地在府中迈方步，从容地出入官府。（太守座中聚会时）在座的有几千人，都说我丈夫出色。"

The sun rises from the southeast, shining on the small building of the Qin family. The Qin family has a beautiful daughter named Luofu. Luofu is skilled in raising silkworms and picking mulberries； one day, she was picking mulberries in south of the city. She used blue silk to make the basket straps and cassia twigs for the basket handles. She wore her hair in a falling-horse style and adorned her ears with pearl earrings. She wore a skirt made of light yellow patterned silk and a short jacket made of purple damask. When passersby saw Luofu, they put down their burdens and stroked their beards, staring at her. Upon seeing Luofu, young men couldn't help but take off their hats and straighten their headbands. Farmers forgot their plowing, and those hoeing forgot their work； upon returning, they blamed each other (for not finishing the farm work), all because they had been captivated by Luofu's beauty.

The governor, riding in his carriage from the south, stopped his five horses, unable to proceed. The governor sent a clerk to ask, "Whose beautiful daughter is this?" The reply was, the Qin family has a beautiful daughter named Luofu. The governor then asked, "How old is Luofu?" "She is not yet twenty, but already over fifteen." The governor then asked Luofu, "Would you like to ride with me?"

Luofu stepped forward and replied, "Governor, how foolish you are! You already have a wife, and I, Luofu, already have a husband!"

"My husband holds a position in the east, with over a thousand men and horses following him. He ranks foremost among them. How can you recognize my husband? He is the high official riding the white horse, followed by a small black horse, with a tail bound in blue silk and a golden bridle on its head. He carries a Lulu sword at his waist, a sword worth thousands of coins. At fifteen, he served as a clerk in the governor's office, at twenty, he became a court official, at thirty, he was the emperor's attendant, and at forty, he became the ruler of a city. He has fair skin and a bit of a beard；he walks calmly with square steps in the mansion and enters and exits the official residence leisurely. At gatherings with thousands of people present, everyone praised my husband as outstanding."

课 后练习

1. 选择题：哀公问孔子"礼"的重要性，孔子认为"礼"的重要性体现在哪些方面？

A. 祭祀天地

B. 社会阶层的区分

C. 亲密关系的维持

D. 所有以上

2. 判断题：孔子提出，只有在各种事务顺利完成后，才能进行丧事的细节讨论和祭祀的安排。

3. 填空题：孔子认为，没有"礼"不能 _____，也无法 _____ 家族与社会的和谐。

4. 简答题：孔子如何解释"礼"的功能以及它如何影响古代社会的日常生活和治理。

5. 讨论题：孔子关于"礼"的观点如何体现了他的哲学思想和他对治国理政的看法。在他的理论中，"礼"是如何促进社会秩序和谐的？

课 文参考翻译

Duke Ai asked Confucius, "What do you think of the propriety (礼) is really like? Why do gentlemen value it so highly?" Confucius replied, "I am just a humble man, how could I possibly understand propriety?" The duke insisted, "No, I would like to hear your views!" Confucius responded, "What I have heard is that among the things that people depend on to survive, propriety is of utmost importance. Without propriety, there is no way to regulate the rituals for the gods of heaven and earth；without propriety, it is impossible to define the roles between ruler and minister, the senior and junior, or the elder and younger；without propriety, there is no way to differentiate the close relationships between men and women, parents and children, brothers, or the relationships through offined and close or distant relations. Therefore, gentlemen regard propriety so important. Then they use their abilities to educate the populace, making them do right things at right time according to propriety. Once successful, they then pay attention to what kind of people use what kind of carvings and sacrificial vessels, wearing what kind of dress, to distinguish the difference between the upper and lower ranks. After these are orderly, they then set different mourning periods for the people, making them prepare the sacrificial vessels, set up offerings, renovate the ancestral temples, conduct solemn rituals at appointed times, arrange family hierarchies. And then gentlemen organize places of residence, simplify clothing, ensure that palaces are unadorned, vehicles are without elaborate decorations, vessels are not intricately carved, and food does not have excessive flavors, in order to share these benefits with the people. This was how the gentlemen of ancient times practiced propriety."

三国两晋南北朝时期的法律（一）

课 前准备

图 8-1　中国国家博物馆：盛世修典——"中国历代绘画大系"成果展
唐·《历代帝王图（曹丕、孙权、刘备）》（阎立本）

东汉末年因黄巾起义导致各地军阀混战，天下呈魏、蜀、吴三足鼎立之势，史称"三国"时期。此后，曹魏强大，灭了刘蜀。但是大权旁落于司马氏。司马炎夺魏平吴，使全国重归一统，史称"西晋"。十多年后"八王之乱"爆发，西北各族乘虚而入，西晋灭亡，残存的政权南迁建康，史称"东晋"。东晋末年权臣刘裕篡位建立"刘宋"，此后又被齐、梁、陈取代，史称"南朝"。与此同时，灭掉西晋的北方少数民族的一支拓跋氏，建立"北魏"，此后分裂为东魏和西魏，不久又分别被北齐、北周所取代，史称"北朝"。[1]

In the late Eastern Han Dynasty, the Yellow Turbans Uprising led to warfare among various warlords, resulting in the division of the Han Empire into three states—Wei, Shu, and Wu—historically known as the "Three Kingdoms" period. Subsequently, Cao Wei became dominant and conquered Liu Shu. However, the state power fell into the hands of the Sima family. Sima Yan, from the Sima family, overthrew Wei and conquered Wu, reuniting the

---

〔1〕 参见朱勇主编：《中国法律史》，中国政法大学出版社 2021 年版，第 120 页。

country under what is known as the "Western Jin" dynasty. More than a decade later, "The War of the Eight Princes" erupted and various ethnic groups from the northwest took advantage of the chaos to overthrow the Western Jin. The remnants of the regime fled south to Jiankang, marking the beginning of what is known as the "Eastern Jin" dynasty. In the late Eastern Jin period, the influential minister Liu Yu usurped the throne to establish the "Liu Song" dynasty, which was subsequently replaced by the Qi, Liang and Chen dynasties, collectively known as the "Southern Dynasties." Meanwhile, a branch of the ethnic groups that overthrew the Western Jin, the Tuoba clan, established the "Northern Wei." The Northern Wei later split into the Eastern Wei and Western Wei, which were soon replaced by the Northern Qi and Northern Zhou, respectively, continuing the historical period known as the "Northern Dynasties."

 生词表

序号	生词	词性	汉语拼音	英文解释
1	黄巾起义	*proper n.*	Huáng jīn Qǐ yì	Yellow Turbans Uprising
2	军阀	*n.*	jūn fá	warlord
3	三足鼎立	*idm.*	sān zú dǐng lì	tripartite confrontation
4	曹魏	*proper n.*	Cáo Wèi	a state in the Three Kingdoms
5	刘蜀	*proper n.*	Liú Shǔ	a state in the Three Kingdoms
6	司马氏	*proper n.*	Sī mǎ shì	Sima clan
7	司马炎	*proper n.*	Sī mǎ Yán	Emperor Wu of Jin
8	八王之乱	*proper n.*	Bā Wáng zhī Luàn	The War of Eight Princes
9	建康	*proper n.*	Jiàn kāng	ancient city in China
10	权臣	*n.*	quán chén	powerful official
11	篡位	*v.*	cuàn wèi	usurp the throne

续表

序号	生词	词性	汉语拼音	英文解释
12	宋	*proper n.*	Sòng	Liu Song dynasty
13	齐	*proper n.*	Qí	Qi dynasty
14	梁	*proper n.*	Liáng	Liang dynasty
15	陈	*proper n.*	Chén	Chen dynasty
16	南朝	*proper n.*	Nán Cháo	Southern Dynasties
17	拓跋氏	*proper n.*	Tuò bá shì	Tuoba clan，founders of Northern Wei
18	北朝	*proper n.*	Běi Cháo	Northern Dynasties
19	东魏	*proper n.*	Dōng Wèi	Eastern Wei dynasty
20	西魏	*proper n.*	Xī Wèi	Western Wei dynasty
21	北齐	*proper n.*	Běi Qí	Northern Qi dynasty
22	北周	*proper n.*	Běi Zhōu	Northern Zhou dynasty

 读

　　三国两晋南北朝时期，政权交替频繁。统治者为了在对峙中获得生存与发展，在政治上多所改易，整个社会的思想层面也发生了许多变化。这些变化表现在法律层面，最显著的是立法思想的变化，立法活动频繁，律学思想活跃，使得法律制度有很大的发展，为之后隋朝以及唐朝法律制度的完善奠定了基础。自从西汉汉武帝"罢黜百家，独尊儒术"之后，儒家思想正式成为官方哲学，对中国传统法律制度和法律思想产生重大影响。然而，儒家宣扬的纲常礼教在被统治阶级使用的过程中逐渐僵化，烦冗刻板的教条禁锢了人们的思想，人们开始探索纠正儒家固化的经学教义的办法，以此来解决实际问题。随着汉王朝的灭亡，正统儒家思想受到挑战，并在魏晋南北朝时期有了新的发展。公元220年，曹丕建立魏朝，之后蜀、吴相继建国，历史进入三国鼎立时期。[1]

曹操性格轻佻而不庄重，喜欢音乐，常有歌舞表演者陪伴在侧，经常从白天玩到夜晚。他穿着轻薄的绡纱衣物，自己佩戴一个小巾囊，用来装手帕和一些小物件，有时会戴着软帽接见宾客。与人交谈时，他言谈诙谐，毫不隐瞒，高兴时大笑不止，甚至笑到头埋进杯盘里，饭菜也常常弄脏了头巾和帽子。曹操常怠慢失礼到这种程度。

图 8-2　河南博物院：曹魏·正始石经

然而，曹操执行法律非常严厉。如果有将领的谋略超过了他的，他就会立即借故用法律处罚他们；对于旧日的朋友和仇敌都同样毫不留情。他对那些被处死的人，常常边流泪边表示哀悼和痛苦，但终究没有放过一个人。

---

〔1〕 参见朱勇主编：《中国法律史》，中国政法大学出版社 2021 年版，第 120 页。

初期，袁忠担任沛相，曾试图依法治罪曹操。沛国的桓邵也曾轻视曹操。当曹操在兖州时，陈留的边让对曹操的言论颇有侵犯之意，曹操于是杀死了边让，并灭其全族。袁忠和桓邵都逃难至交州，曹操派使者命交州太守处死他们全族。桓邵前来自首，在庭中磕头谢罪时，曹操问他："跪下就能免死吗？"最终还是将他杀死。

曹操曾在行军途中经过麦田，命令"士卒不得踏坏麦子，违者死"。骑兵都下马步行，小心翼翼地避开麦田。然而曹操的马却跳进了麦田中，他命主簿商议如何处罚，主簿根据《春秋》的义理认为刑罚不施加于尊贵之人。曹操说："制定法律却自己违反，怎么能领导部下？不过，我作为军队统帅，不能自杀，请允许我自行惩罚。"然后他拔剑割下自己的头发放在地上。

 原文参考

《三国志·魏书·武帝纪》（节选）：曹瞒传曰：太祖为人佻易无威重，好音乐，倡优在侧，常以日达夕。被服轻绡，身自佩小鞶囊，以盛手巾细物，时或冠帢帽以见宾客。每与人谈论，戏弄言诵，尽无所隐，及欢悦大笑，至以头没杯案中，肴膳皆沾污巾帻，其轻易如此。

然持法峻刻，诸将有计画胜出己者，随以法诛之，及故人旧怨，亦皆无馀。其所刑杀，辄对之垂涕嗟痛之，终无所活。

初，袁忠为沛相，尝欲以法治太祖，沛国桓邵亦轻之，及在兖州，陈留边让言议颇侵太祖，太祖杀让，族其家。忠、邵俱避难交州，太祖遣使就太守止燮尽族之。桓邵得出首，拜谢于庭中，太祖谓曰："跪可解死邪！"遂杀之。

尝出军，行经麦中，令"士卒无败麦，犯者死"。骑士皆下马，持麦以相付，于是太祖马腾入麦中，敕主簿议罪；主簿对以春秋之义，罚不加于尊。太祖曰："制法而自犯之，何以帅下？然孤为军帅，不可自杀，请自刑。"因援剑割发以置地。

生词表

序号	生词	词性	汉语拼音	英文解释
1	轻佻	adj.	qīng tiāo	frivolous
2	绡纱	n.	xiāo shā	silk gauze
3	巾囊	n.	jīn náng	small pouch
4	诙谐	adj.	huī xié	humorous
5	怠慢	v.	dài màn	neglect, disregard
6	严厉	adj.	yán lì	strict, severe
7	谋略	n.	móu luè	strategy, tactics
8	借故	phr.	jiè gù	find some excuse
9	桓邵	proper n.	Huán Shào	a person's name
10	边让	proper n.	Biān Ràng	a person's name
11	灭族	v.	miè zú	exterminate one's family/clan
12	自首	phr.	zì shǒu	surrender oneself
13	谢罪	phr.	xiè zuì	apologize for a crime
14	士卒	n.	shì zú	soldiers, troops
15	麦田	n.	mài tián	wheat field
16	主簿	n.	zhǔ bù	official in charge of paperwork
17	春秋	proper n.	Chūn qiū	a book's name
18	尊贵	adj.	zūn guì	noble, distinguished
19	统帅	n.	tǒng shuài	commander-in-chief
20	惩罚	v.	chéng fá	punish

 点汉字【狱】

狱，源于囚。汉代《急就篇》记载："皋陶造狱法律存"。指皋陶作为东夷的部落首领，制刑造狱，成为中国历史上关于监狱的起源。

狱的本义从犬，二犬相守为"狱"。夏朝时，开始用圈养牛羊的土"牢"，来关押俘虏和奴隶。"牢"与"狱"，功能是不同的。"牢"从牛，闲也，只负责普通关押。"狱"从犬，二犬相守，更重威慑与惩戒。明律开始称"狱"为"监"，清朝合并为"监狱"。明律中，"由门而逃曰脱监，逾墙而逃曰越狱"。

图 8-3 "狱"字篆刻（王琦 刻）

 汉字拓展

序号	词汇	汉语拼音	英文解释	例句
1	监狱	jiān yù	prison	他因为重罪被判处在监狱服刑五年。
2	狱警	yù jǐng	prison guard	狱警负责确保监狱的安全和秩序。
3	狱友	yù yǒu	fellow prisoner	在监狱里，他和一个狱友成为好朋友。
4	出狱	chū yù	release from prison	他终于出狱了，可以开始新的生活。
5	狱卒	yù zú	jailer	狱卒在过去常常被描述为残酷无情。
6	狱长	yù zhǎng	prison warden	狱长对于整个监狱的运行负有重大责任。
7	劫狱	jié yù	jailbreak	劫狱事件发生后，当局加强了监狱的安全措施。

化知识【《三国演义》】

　　章回体小说《三国演义》，是元末明初小说家罗贯中在有关三国故事的宋元话本、戏曲和轶事传闻的基础上，根据陈寿的《三国志》及裴松之注解以及民间三国故事传说、经过艺术加工创作而成的长篇历史演义小说。又名《三国志演义》《三国志通俗演义》。它与《西游记》《水浒传》《红楼梦》并称为"中国古典四大名著"。

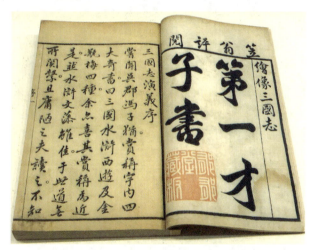

图 8-4　国家典籍博物馆：清·《笠翁批阅三国志演义》郁郁斋刻本

　　从全书架构来看，《三国演义》大致分为"黄巾起义""董卓之乱""群雄逐鹿""三国鼎立""三国归晋"五大部分，描写了从东汉末年到西晋初年近百年的战争历史风云，特别是东汉末年的群雄割据混战和曹魏、蜀汉、东吴三国之间的政治和军事斗争，以及最终司马炎一统三国、建立晋朝的故事。它塑造了一群叱咤风云的三国英雄人物。

　　《三国演义》成书后，有多个版本流传于世，到了明末清初，毛宗岗对《三国演义》整顿回目、修正文辞、改换诗文，该版本也成为诸多版本中水平最高、流传最广的版本。

　　《三国演义》作为中国文学史上第一部章回体小说，是历史演义小说的开山之作，明清时期甚至有"第一才子书"之称。后世文学作品中，取材于该书的各类题材不胜枚举。它的影响力之巨，以至于其艺术性一定程度上盖过了历史的真实。

法 治文物【"獬豸"博物馆（六）】

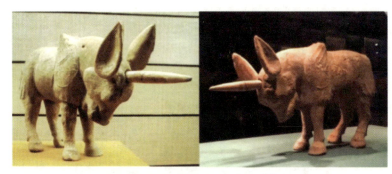

图8-4　北朝·陶质独角兽[1]

经 典阅读

《三国演义》第一回：宴桃园豪杰三结义　斩黄巾英雄首立功（节选）[2]

词曰：滚滚长江东逝水，浪花淘尽英雄。是非成败转头空：青山依旧在，几度夕阳红。白发渔樵江渚上，惯看秋月春风。一壶浊酒喜相逢：古今多少事，都付笑谈中。

话说天下大势，分久必合，合久必分：周末七国分争，并入于秦；及秦灭之后，楚、汉分争，又并入于汉；汉朝自高祖斩白蛇而起义，一统天下，后来光武中兴，传至献帝，遂分为三国。推其致乱之由，殆始于桓、灵二帝。桓帝禁锢善类，崇信宦官。及桓帝崩，灵帝即位，大将军窦武、太傅陈蕃，共相辅佐；时有宦官曹节等弄权，窦武、陈蕃谋诛之，机事不密，反为所害，

---

〔1〕　参见李雪梅：《谜一样的独角兽（一）》，载《中国法律评论》2021年第2期。

〔2〕　选自（明）罗贯中：《三国演义》，人民文学出版社2019年版，第1~2页。

中涓自此愈横。

建宁二年四月望日，帝御温德殿。方升座，殿角狂风骤起，只见一条大青蛇，从梁上飞将下来，蟠于椅上。帝惊倒，左右急救入宫，百官俱奔避。须臾，蛇不见了。忽然大雷大雨，加以冰雹，落到半夜方止，坏却房屋无数。建宁四年二月，洛阳地震；又海水泛溢，沿海居民，尽被大浪卷入海中。光和元年，雌鸡化雄。六月朔，黑气十余丈，飞入温德殿中。秋七月，有虹现于玉堂，五原山岸，尽皆崩裂。种种不祥，非止一端。帝下诏问群臣以灾异之由，议郎蔡邕上疏，以为蜺堕鸡化，乃妇寺干政之所致，言颇切直。帝览奏叹息，因起更衣。曹节在后窃视，悉宣告左右；遂以他事陷邕于罪，放归田里。后张让、赵忠、封谞、段珪、曹节、侯览、蹇硕、程旷、夏恽、郭胜十人朋比为奸，号为"十常侍"。帝尊信张让，呼为"阿父"。朝政日非，以致天下人心思乱，盗贼蜂起。[1]

 参考译文

Verse goes: The rolling river flows east, washing away all heroes. Right and wrong, success and failure, turn to emptiness in a moment. The green mountains still stand, witness to how many red sunsets. White-haired fishers and woodcutters on the river isles, accustomed to watching the autumn moon and spring breeze. A pot of cloudy wine for joyous meetings: countless affairs of the past and present, all discussed with laughter.

The narrative says: The general trend of the world is that separation leads to union and union leads to separation. In the end of the Zhou dynasty, the seven states contended and were unified into Qin; after the fall of Qin, Chu and Han contended, then were unified into Han. The Han dynasty started with Emperor Gaozu rising in

---

〔1〕 东汉桓帝刘志、灵帝刘宏在位的 40 余年，朝政腐败、宦官专权、民不聊生。巨鹿（今河北省邢台市平乡县）人张角于汉灵帝中平元年（公元 184 年）发动了黄巾起义。起义军逼近幽州，太守刘焉出榜招贤，刘备、关羽、张飞结伴同去投军，首战获胜并救出董卓。小说起始的这首词为明代三大才子之一的杨慎所写，该词借叙述历史兴亡抒发人生感慨，读来荡气回肠，折射出高远的意境和深邃的人生哲理。本回的重点在桃园三结义，这份兄弟情义贯穿了他们一生。

rebellion after slaying a white serpent, and unified the land. Later, Emperor Guang-wu revived the Han, passing the throne to Emperor Xian, which eventually led to the division into three kingdoms. The cause of the chaos traced back mostly to Emperors Huan and Ling. Emperor Huan suppressed the good and trusted eunuchs. Upon his death, Emperor Ling ascended, assisted by Grand General Dou Wu and Imperial Tutor Chen Fan. Eunuchs like Cao Jie manipulated power; Dou Wu and Chen Fan plotted their execution, but the plan leaked, turning deadly for them instead, and eunuch influence only grew stronger thereafter.

In the second year of Jian Ning in the fourth month on the day of the full moon, the Emperor was in the Wende Hall. Just as he ascended the throne, a sudden gust from the corner of the hall blew in, and a large blue serpent flew down from the beam, coiling on the chair. The Emperor collapsed in fright; the attendants rushed to help him into the palace, and all the officials fled. Soon, the serpent vanished. Suddenly, there was a great thunderstorm with hail, which lasted until midnight, destroying countless houses. In the fourth year of Jian Ning in February, an earthquake struck Luoyang, and a tidal wave swept all the coastal inhabitants into the sea. In the first year of Guang He, a hen turned into a rooster. On the first day of June, a black mist more than thirty feet high flew into the Wende Hall. In July of autumn, a rainbow appeared over the Yutang Hall, and the banks of Mount Wuyuan all crumbled. Various omens appeared, not just one or two. The Emperor issued an edict to consult his ministers about the cause of these disasters. Scholar-official Cai Yong submitted a memorial suggesting that these strange occurrences were caused by the interference of women in government, his words quite direct. The Emperor read the memorial and sighed, then rose to change his clothing. Cao Jie secretly watched him, reported everything to others, and then used other matters to frame Cai Yong, exiling him to the countryside. Later, Zhang Rang, Zhao Zhong, Feng Xu, Duan Gui, Cao Jie, Hou Lan, Jian Shuo, Cheng Kuang, Xia Yun, and Guo Sheng, ten eunuchs known collectively as the "Ten Attendants," schemed together. The Emperor deeply trusted Zhang Rang, calling him "Father." As the court politics deteriorated day by day, it led to chaos across the land, with thieves and rebels rising everywhere.

课 后练习

1. 选择题：曹操在个人生活中的哪一方面与他作为统治者时的行为对比最为鲜明？

A. 喜欢音乐与对音乐家的批评。

B. 穿着轻薄衣物与对服装的规范要求。

C. 在接见宾客时轻佻的态度与在法律实施上的严格。

D. 与人诙谐交谈与对反对者的宽容。

2. 判断题：曹操处罚旧日朋友和仇敌时，会根据个人感情从轻发落。

3. 填空题：在行军途中，曹操特别命令士卒_____，以体现其对法律的尊重。

4. 简答题：曹操如何处理自己的违法行为？

5. 论述题：曹操在法律执行中表现出的公正性和其对统治的影响。

课 文参考翻译

Cao Cao had a light-hearted and unserious demeanor; he enjoyed music and was often accompanied by performers of song and dance, having fun from dawn to dusk. He wore light silk clothing and carried a small pouch for handkerchiefs and other small items, occasionally donning a soft hat when meeting guests. In conversation, he was witty and unreserved, often laughing uncontrollably, even burying his head in the table in mirth, frequently staining his headscarf and hat with food in such casual displays.

However, Cao Cao enforced the law with great severity. If any general's plan surpassed his, he would immediately punish them legally on some excuse; he was equally merciless towards old friends and foes alike. As for those executed, he often wept and expressed sorrow and pain, yet he never spared anyone.

Initially, Yuan Zhong served as the magistrate of Pei and had once tried to declare Cao Cao's guilty by law. Huan Shao of Pei also looked down on Cao Cao. When Cao was in Yanzhou, Bian Rang from Chenliu made comments that were offensive to Cao Cao, leading Cao to kill him and exterminate his family. Yuan Zhong and Huan Shao both fled to Jiaozhou, where Cao Cao sent an envoy to order the governor there to execute their entire families. When Huan Shao apologized to Cao Cao by kneeling in court, Cao asked him, "Do you think kneeling can save you from death?" He then had him killed.

Once, while his army was marching through a wheat field, Cao Cao ordered, "Soldiers must not trample the wheat; violators will be put to death." The cavalry dismounted and walked carefully to avoid damaging the wheat. However, Cao Cao's horse jumped into the wheat field, and he ordered his registrar to discuss the punishment. According to the principles of the *Spring and Autumn Annals*, penalties should not apply to the nobility. Cao Cao remarked, "How can I lead if I violate the laws I set? However, as the commander, I cannot kill myself; please allow me to punish myself." He then drew his sword and cut off his hair, placing it on the ground.

第九课

三国两晋南北朝时期的法律（二）

课 前准备

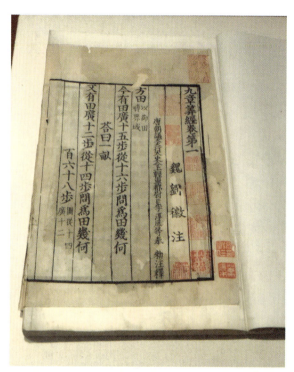

图 9-1　国家典籍博物馆：晋·九章算经　（刘徽）

　　魏晋时期，世族门阀地位不断上升，政治地位不断膨胀，形成了以血缘家族为基础的特定社会群体。据统计，有"高门""势家""世家""世族"等28种称谓，其中最为人所通用的是"士族"。魏晋南北朝的世家大族虽然人数仅占总人数很小的一部分，但由于他们往往占据国家政权中的高位，在社会上又具有很大的影响，因而成为这一时期具有代表性的家族。他们以高贵血统为说辞，推行不与寒门、贫民通婚交往的政策。在经济上的"品官占田荫客制"和政治上所确立的"九品中正制"的双重作用影响下，门阀世族与国家统治阶层开始融为一体并控制了国家政权，通过制定法律将各种经济与政治特权规范化与法律化。此外，门阀世族阶层在思想层面的一个显著特质即重视儒家经学的发展。他们直接参与法律的制定，进一步将儒家的宗法观念、礼仪习俗和道德观念以法律的形式固定了下来，成为重要的法律原则与法律观念，实现了法律与礼义道德的融合。儒家思想与法律制度的结合，既是门阀世族地位的重要依托与保障，也是法律儒家化的具体呈现。[1]

During the Wei and Jin periods, the status of aristocratic clans continuously rose, inflating their political influence and forming a specific social group based on kinship. According to records, there were 28 titles such as "high gates," "powerful families," "noble families," and "clans," among which "Shizu (aristocratic clans)" was the most commonly used. Despite constituting only a small fraction of the total population, these great families of the Wei, Jin, Northern, and Southern Dynasties often occupied high positions in the state's governance and exerted significant social influence, thus becoming the representative families of this era. They used their noble lineage as justification for policies that prevented marriage and social interaction with the lower classes and the impoverished. Under the dual influence of the "ranking officials based on their land and patronage system" in the economy and the "Nine Rank System" in politics, these aristocratic families merged with the ruling class and seized control of state power, standardizing various economic and political privileges through legislation. Furthermore, a significant characteristic of the aristocratic families was their emphasis on the development of Confucian classics. They were directly involved in legislating and solidified Confucian clan principles, etiquette, and moral concepts into legal forms, thus becoming key legal principles and concepts and achieving an integration of law with Confucian ethics and morals. This merger of Confucian thought and legal system not only supported the status of the aristocratic families but also manifested in the Confucianization of the law.

---

〔1〕 参见朱勇主编：《中国法律史》，中国政法大学出版社 2021 年版，第 122 页。

生词表

序号	生词	词性	汉语拼音	英文解释
1	士族	*n.*	shì zú	aristocratic clans
2	门阀	*n.*	mén fá	influential families
3	血缘	*n.*	xuè yuán	blood relation
4	势家	*n.*	shì jiā	powerful families
5	寒门	*n.*	hán mén	poor families
6	贫民	*n.*	pín mín	poor people
7	品官占田荫客制	*proper n.*	Pǐn guān Zhàn tián Yìn kè Zhì	system of guaranteeing the economic privileges of the aristocracy and the bureaucracy
8	九品中正制	*proper n.*	Jiǔ pǐn Zhōng zhèng Zhì	a method of selecting officials
9	高贵	*adj.*	gāo guì	noble
10	礼仪	*n.*	lǐ yí	etiquette
11	道德	*n.*	dào dé	morality
12	法律化	*v.*	fǎ lǜ huà	legalize
13	宗法	*n.*	zōng fǎ	clan law
14	儒家化	*n.*	rú jiā huà	Confucianization
15	重视	*v.*	zhòng shì	value
16	代表性	*n.*	dài biǎo xìng	representativeness

 读

　　在正统儒家思想的影响下，经过门阀世族的熏染和努力，法律儒家化在魏晋南北朝时期到达高峰，中国传统法的伦理特点在这一时期的法律中得到了充分表达。主要表现在以下几个方面：其一，以伦理为中心，强化法律对儒家伦理的保护；其二，以血缘和官阶等为基础，强化对伦理等级的维护；其三，以家族为本位，严惩"不孝"，维护家长特权。

课 文

　　在中国的古代封建社会中，法律制度是维护统治秩序的重要工具，其中"十恶"罪名在历史上占有重要地位。这一概念源于西汉时期，随着时间的推移，这一概念逐渐发展并扩展为具体的法律条款。北齐时期，法律制度得到了重要的发展。公元564年，即北齐河清三年，尚书令和赵郡王等人奏定齐律十二篇，史称《北齐律》，系统列出了十条重罪，这些罪行被视为对封建秩序的严重威胁，犯有这些罪行的人不得受到宽赦的处理。

图 9-2　甘肃敦煌：莫高窟壁画

此后随着佛教在中国的广泛传播和影响力的增强，隋朝时期的封建统治者开始将佛教中的道德观念融入法律体系。公元 581 年，隋朝建立之初，隋文帝开创性地将佛教的"十恶"罪名引入《开皇律》，正式替代了《北齐律》中的重罪十条。至唐朝，《唐律疏议》进一步明确到了"十恶"罪的具体法律内容和适用范围，这些规定具体说明了各种罪行对封建社会稳定的威胁程度，反映了封建社会对各种行为的道德和法律评价。在封建社会中，这些罪行不仅是法律上的重罪，也是道德上的大忌，涉及了神权、君权、父权和夫权，是维护封建秩序的关键。

　　由于"十恶"罪直接危害到了封建社会的核心价值和权威，自隋代《开皇律》首次确立这一法律概念以来，历代封建法典均将其列为不可赦免的重罪。这一法律概念的严格性和持续性显示了封建法律在维护统治秩序方面的决心和力度，也反映了封建统治者利用法律手段来强化自身统治的策略。因此，"十恶不赦"成为民间广为流传的说法，深刻影响了人们的行为和思想。

 生词表

序号	生词	词性	汉语拼音	英文解释
1	封建	n.	fēng jiàn	feudalism
2	秩序	n.	zhì xù	order, sequence
3	概念	n.	gài niàn	concept
4	条款	n.	tiáo kuǎn	clause, provision
5	重罪	n.	zhòng zuì	serious crime, felony
6	宽赦	v.	kuān shè	amnesty
7	传播	v.	chuán bō	spread, disseminate
8	影响力	n.	yǐng xiǎng lì	influence
9	融入	v.	róng rù	integrate, merge
10	开创性	n.	kāi chuàng xìng	pioneering, innovation
11	替代	v.	tì dài	replace

续表

序号	生词	词性	汉语拼音	英文解释
12	稳定	*adj.*	wěn dìng	stable
13	适用范围	*phr.*	shì yòng fàn wéi	scope of application
14	大忌	*n.*	dà jì	taboo
15	维护	*v.*	wéi hù	maintain，uphold
16	父权	*n.*	fù quán	paternal authority
17	神权	*n.*	shén quán	theocratic authority
18	持续性	*n.*	chí xù xìng	continuity，persistence
19	尚书令	*n.*	shàng shū lìng	an official title in ancient Chinese government
20	赵郡王	*n.*	Zhào jùn wáng	title of a noble in ancient China
21	赦免	*v.*	shè miǎn	pardon，forgive

重 点汉字【禁】

图 9-3 "禁"字篆刻（王琦 刻）

　　禁，汉语一级字，读作 jīn 或 jìn，会意字。"示"字部，本义指禁忌。表示"相违背"，引申为"错误的"，与"是"相对，又由此引申为"反对、责难"。"禁"的基本字义是"受得住"，如禁不起、弱不禁风，后引申词义为"制止"、不能做法律或习惯上不允许的事，如犯禁、违禁品，当词义扩大以后，亦可表示"拘押"，如囚禁、禁闭，古时，"禁"也用来表示帝王所在的地方，如禁宫、禁苑，也把专门保卫京城或宫廷的军队称为"禁军"。

 汉字拓展

序号	词汇	汉语拼音	英文解释	例句
1	禁止	jìn zhǐ	prohibit	这个公园禁止吸烟。
2	禁忌	jìn jì	taboo	在很多文化中，谈论死亡是一个禁忌。
3	禁区	jìn qū	restricted area	这个区域是军事禁区，禁止进入。
4	禁锢	jìn gù	confine	他感觉自己被传统观念禁锢了。
5	禁烟	jìn yān	no smoking	火车站内设有禁烟区。
6	禁令	jìn lìng	ban	政府发布了一个新的环保禁令。
7	禁欲	jìn yù	ascetic	他选择了禁欲的生活方式。
8	解禁	jiě jìn	lift a ban	政府已对某些进口商品解禁。
9	禁食	jìn shí	fast	宗教仪式要求他们全天禁食。
10	禁闭	jìn bì	confinement	因为违反规定，他被关了三天禁闭。
11	禁赛	jìn sài	suspend from game	运动员因违规被禁赛四场。
12	禁用	jìn yòng	disable	这款软件的旧版本已被禁用。
13	禁书	jìn shū	banned book	这部小说曾被列为禁书。

 化知识【王羲之与《兰亭集序》】

《兰亭集序》，通称《兰亭序》或《禊帖》，是晋代书法家王羲之的杰作，被誉为"天下第一行书"，体现了晋代书法的巅峰成就。这篇作品共324字，字字珠圆玉润，每一个"之"字均独具匠心，显示了作者的高超技艺。

永和九年（公元353年）春，王羲之与他的儿子王凝之、王徽之、王操之、王献之，以及孙统、李充、孙绰、谢安等一众文人雅士，在会稽山阴的兰亭举行了一场别开生面的集会。这次集会中产生了37首诗歌，后来编纂成《兰亭诗》。《兰亭集序》即是王羲之为这本诗集所作的序言，他用精心挑选的鼠须笔和蚕茧纸，从聚会的盛况着笔，描绘了"茂林修竹、清流激湍"的自然景致，及"天朗气清，惠风和畅"的宜人气候。随后转入深沉的哀愁，反思人生短暂和欢乐时光易逝，表达了对时光流转的感慨。王羲之在文中并没有简单宣扬"及时行乐"的思想，而是对庄子的生死观进行了深刻的思考和辩驳。这篇序语言流畅自然，没有刻意雕琢，运用了骈散结合的文风，灵活自如，被后世誉为不朽名篇。

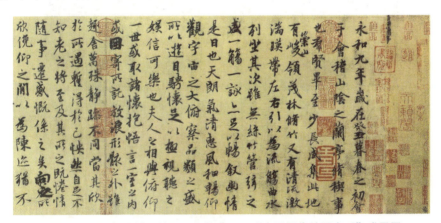

图 9-4　中国国家博物馆：盛世修典——"中国历代绘画大系"成果展
《兰亭序》神龙本（局部）

唐太宗对《兰亭集序》情有独钟，彼时王羲之的真迹传到了王羲之七世孙智永的徒弟辨才手中。辨才因不忍割爱，未将此作品交予唐太宗。后来，唐太宗派人用计取得了这部作品，并将其作为殉葬品。宋代陆游在他的诗《跋冯氏兰亭》中对此表示哀叹："茧纸藏昭陵，千载不复见。"有史料记载，唐太宗的昭陵在唐末五代时被盗，但《兰亭集序》并未在被盗之列，因此普遍认为其可能尚在唐高宗与武则天合葬的乾陵中。

 治文物【十二时神】

图9-5　北朝、唐·十二时神（生肖俑）[1]

经 典阅读

《兰亭集序》

永和九年，岁在癸丑，暮春之初，会于会稽山阴之兰亭，修禊事也。群贤毕至，少长咸集。此地有崇山峻岭，茂林修竹，又有清流激湍，映带左右，引以为流觞曲水，列坐其次。虽无丝竹管弦之盛，一觞一咏，亦足以畅叙幽情。

是日也，天朗气清，惠风和畅。仰观宇宙之大，俯察品类之盛，所以游目骋怀，足以极视听之娱，信可乐也。

夫人之相与，俯仰一世。或取诸怀抱，悟言一室之内；或因寄所托，放

---

[1] 参见《北朝、唐·十二时神（生肖俑）》，载中国政法大学中华法制文明虚拟博物馆，https://flqj.cupl.edu.cn/info/1072/4056.htm，最后访问日期：2024 年 9 月 27 日。

浪形骸之外。虽趣舍万殊，静躁不同，当其欣于所遇，暂得于己，快然自足，不知老之将至。及其所之既倦，情随事迁，感慨系之矣。向之所欣，俯仰之间，已为陈迹，犹不能不以之兴怀，况修短随化，终期于尽。古人云："死生亦大矣。"岂不痛哉！

每揽昔人兴感之由，若合一契，未尝不临文嗟悼，不能喻之于怀。固知一死生为虚诞，齐彭殇为妄作。后之视今，亦由今之视昔，悲夫！故列叙时人，录其所述，虽世殊事异，所以兴怀，其致一也。后之揽者，亦将有感于斯文。

参考译文

永和九年，正是癸丑之年，三月上旬，我们相聚在会稽郡山阴城的兰亭，为了做祭礼。众多有才干的人汇聚于此，长者与青年才俊都在。兰亭这个地方有高峻的山峰，茂盛的树林，修长的竹子；也有清澈湍急的溪流，辉映环绕在亭子的四周，我们引溪水作为流觞的曲水，排列坐在曲水两边，虽然没有演奏音乐，但喝点酒，作点诗，也足以畅快叙述深厚的感情了。

这一天，天气晴朗，和风温暖。抬头可以看到浩渺宇宙，低头则见世间众多万物，因此舒展眼界，开阔胸怀，完全能够极尽视听的欢娱，实在很快乐。

人与人相互交往，很快便度过一生。有的人从自己的思想中感悟些许，在居所（跟朋友）面对面地交谈；有的人通过寄情于自己爱好的事物，不受任何约束地放纵生活。虽然各有各的爱好，安静与躁动各不相同，但当他们对所接触的事物感到高兴时，都会暂时感到自得、快乐与满足，不知衰老将要到来。等到对得到或喜爱的东西已经厌倦，感情随着事物的变化而变化，感慨就随之产生。过去所喜欢的东西，转瞬间，已经成为旧迹，且因它引发心中的感触，况且寿命长短，听凭造化，最后归结于终。古人说："生死毕竟是件大事啊。"怎么能不让人悲痛呢！

每当看到前人所发感慨的原因，其缘由像一张符契那样相和，总难免要在读前人文章时叹息哀伤，无法释怀。虽然知道把死和生等同起来的说法是不真实的，把长寿和短命等同起来的说法是虚妄的。后人看待今人，也就像今人看待前人，可悲呀。所以记下此时与会的人，录下他们所作的诗篇。纵使时代变了，事情不同了，但触发人们情怀的原因，他们的思想情趣是一样的。后世的读者，也将对这次集会的诗文有所感悟。

In the ninth year of Yonghe, which was a Gui Chou year, in early March, we gathered at the Lanting in Shanyin of Kuaiji Prefecture for a ceremonial rite. Many talented individuals assembled here, including esteemed elders and young talents. The Lanting is surrounded by lofty mountains, lush forests, and slender bamboos; it also features clear, rushing streams that mirror the surroundings of the pavilion. We drew water from the stream for our wine-drinking rite, arranging ourselves along its banks. Although there was no music played, the wine and poetry sufficed to deeply convey our emotions.

On this day, the weather was clear, and a gentle breeze warmed us. Looking up, we saw the vast universe; gazing down, we observed myriad things of the world, thus broadening our horizons and our spirits, fully indulging in the joys of sight and sound, truly a delightful experience.

Interactions among people swiftly pass a lifetime. Some gain insights from their own thoughts, engaging in face-to-face conversations in their dwellings; others express their spirits through things they are passionate about, indulging in life without restraint. While everyone has their preferences, whether serene or restless, the pleasure they derive from their experiences brings temporary contentment and joy, unaware of the impending old age. Once tired of cherished possessions or when feelings change with circumstances, reflections arise. What was once loved quickly becomes a relic of the past, evoking emotional responses, particularly as life's duration is subject to fate, ultimately concluding with death. The ancients said, "Life and death are indeed great matters," how could it not evoke sorrow!

Whenever we encounter reasons for ancient sentiments, and their causes align like a tally, it's inevitable for me to feel melancholic and unable to let go while reading their writings. Although the notion that equates life with death is unreal, and that long and short lives are the same is illusory. Future generations will view us as we view those before us; how pitiful! Thus, I recorded the participants and their poems right now. Even if times change and circumstances differ, the triggers of human emotions and their artistic tastes remain the same. Future readers will also find resonance in the poetry from this gathering.

课 后练习

1. 选择题：在中国古代法律史上，"十恶"罪名最早出现在哪个朝代的法律文献中？

A. 西汉

B. 北齐

C. 隋朝

D. 唐朝

2. 判断题：隋文帝将佛教"十恶"的道德观念融入《开皇律》中，是为了替代北齐关于重罪十条的法律体系。

3. 填空题：在公元 ___ 年，北齐法律文献首次系统地列出了"十恶"罪名，这些罪名被视为对封建秩序的严重威胁。

4. 简答题：为什么"十恶"罪名在封建社会中被视为重罪，这涉及了封建统治者哪些方面的权力？

5. 讨论题："十恶不赦"对于维护封建统治秩序的影响。你认为这种法律的严格性和持续性是如何影响民众行为和思想的？

课 文参考翻译

In ancient Chinese feudal society, the legal system was an essential tool for maintaining the order of rule, with the concept of the "Ten Abominations" holding a significant historical position. Initially emerging during the Western Han Dynasty, this concept gradually evolved and expanded into specific legal provisions over time. During the Northern Qi period, the legal system underwent significant development. In the year AD 564, during the third year of Heqing, the Imperial Secretary and the Prince of Zhao Prefecture, among others, formalized the Qi Laws in twelve volumes, known as "Laws of Northern Qi" in history. These laws systematically listed ten grave offenses considered severe threats to feudal order, and individuals guilty of these offenses were not eligible for amnesty.

As Buddhism spread widely and gained influence in China, feudal rulers of the Sui Dynasty began integrating Buddhist moral concepts into the legal framework. In AD 581, at the inception of the Sui Dynasty, Emperor Wen innovatively incorporated the Buddhist concept of the "Ten Abominations" into the "Kaihuang Code," formally replacing the ten grave crimes listed in the "Laws of Northern Qi." By the Tang Dynasty, the "Commentary on Law Codes of Tang Dynasty" further clarified the specific legal content and application of the "Ten Abominations," detailing the extent to which various offenses threatened the stability of feudal society and reflecting the moral and legal judgments of the feudal society on various behaviors. In feudal society, these offenses were not only severe crimes legally but also major moral taboos, involving the powers of the divine, the emperor, the father, and the husband, crucial for upholding the feudal order.

Since the "Ten Abominations" directly endangered the core values and authority of feudal society, from the establishment of this legal concept in the "Kaihuang Code" of the Sui Dynasty, subsequent feudal legal codes consistently classified it as an unpardonable severe crime. The strictness and persistence of this legal concept demonstrated the determination and intensity of feudal law in maintaining order, reflecting how feudal rulers used legal means to strengthen their rule. Consequently, the concept of "unforgivable Ten Abominations" became a widely known saying among the people, profoundly influencing their behavior and thoughts.

三国两晋南北朝时期的法律（三）

图 10-1 陕西历史博物馆：西魏·独孤信多面体煤精组印

三国两晋南北朝时期，律学成果丰富，先后为封建法典所吸收。这一时期的律典结构体例发生了很大变化，篇目篇幅趋于合理，律典体例结构也更加科学。曹魏时期编定的《新律》共 18 篇，与"汉律六十篇"相比，大大减少。晋朝的《泰始律》共 20 章，620 条，并正式将"律"与"令"分开，使其既分工又协调，整个律令体系得到大幅精简。《北齐律》在晋律基础上再次进行大的调整，整个律典共 12 篇，较晋律更为精简。

在律典体例结构方面，形成了总则在前、分则在后的体例，为隋唐律《名例》总则在前，《卫禁》《职制》等实体法居中，《捕亡》《断狱》等诉讼程序法律在后的传统律典 12 篇的经典体例打下基础。中国传统律典经过魏晋南北朝数百年的探索，在篇目和体例方面对后世的唐、宋、元、明、清诸朝产生了深远影响。[1]

During the Three Kingdoms, Jin Dynasty, and Southern and Northern Dynasties, the field of jurisprudence achieved rich outcomes, which were subsequently integrated into the feudal legal codes. This period saw signifi-

---

〔1〕 参见朱勇主编：《中国法律史》，中国政法大学出版社 2021 年版，第 123~127 页。

cant changes in the structure and format of legal codes, with more rational organization and a more scientific structure. The "New Laws" compiled in Cao Wei period consisted of 18 sections, has a substantial reduction compared to "Sixty Articles of Han Law". The Jin Dynasty's "Taishi Code" comprised 20 chapters with 620 articles and formally separated "令" （decrees） from "律" （laws）, enhancing both division of labor and coordination within the legal system, significantly streamlining the entire code. "Laws of Northern Qi", building upon the Jin laws, underwent further major adjustments, resulting in a total of 12 chapters, making them even more concise than those of Jin.

In terms of the structure of legal codes, a format was established with general principles at the beginning, followed by specific regulations, laying the groundwork for the classical format of the 12-chapter traditional codes seen in the Sui and Tang laws. The general principles, "Names and Examples" were outlined first, with substantive laws like "Guard and Prohibition" and "Official Systems" in the middle, and procedural laws such as "Pursuit of Escapees" and "Legal Adjudication" at the end. The exploration of Chinese traditional legal codes throughout hundreds of years during the Wei, Jin, and Northern and Southern Dynasties profoundly influenced the legal systems of subsequent dynasties, including the Tang, Song, Yuan, Ming, and Qing.

 生词表

序号	生词	词性	汉语拼音	英文解释
1	律学	*n.*	lǜ xué	jurisprudence
2	律典	*n.*	lǜ diǎn	code of laws
3	篇目	*n.*	piān mù	chapters and sections

续表

序号	生词	词性	汉语拼音	英文解释
4	篇幅	n.	piān fú	length of a document
5	泰始律	proper n.	Tài shǐ Lǜ	laws of the Taishi era
6	分工	v.	fēn gōng	division of labor
7	精简	v.	jīng jiǎn	streamline
8	调整	v.	tiáo zhěng	adjust
9	总则	n.	zǒng zé	general rules
10	分则	n.	fēn zé	specific rules
11	实体法	n.	shí tǐ fǎ	substantive law
12	捕亡	proper n.	Bǔ wáng	the law on arrest of criminals
13	断狱	proper n.	Duàn yù	the law about adjudication
14	律令	n.	lǜ lìng	system of laws and decrees
15	体例	n.	tǐ lì	structure and style
16	名例	proper n.	Míng lì	the law about penal names and examples
17	卫禁	proper n.	Wèi jìn	the law about guards and prohibitions
18	职制	proper n.	Zhí zhì	the law about system of official duties
19	传统律典	phr.	chuán tǒng lǜ diǎn	traditional code of laws
20	探索	v.	tàn suǒ	explore

 导 读

　　魏晋南北朝时期律学的发达，推动了这一时期律令体系的发展，改变了秦汉以来法律形式繁杂、彼此之间难以区别的情况，为隋唐时期古代律令体系发展的高峰准备了条件。

图 10-2　河南博物院：南朝·文吏俑浮雕砖

　　"八议"是中国古代的官员或贵族享受的一种法律特权，源于西周时期的"八辟"制度。三国时期魏明帝制定《新律》时，首次将其写入法典，此后一直是历代法典中一项基本的重要制度。八议者除犯"十恶"的死罪，否则司法机关不能直接审理，必须先将其犯罪事实及应享受特权的理由奏请皇帝，由皇帝交群臣集体商议后，最后由皇帝作出裁决，一般可免除死罪。若犯流刑以下的罪，则可直接减一等处罚。但是犯十恶者不适用八议的规定。

　　"八议"的范围可见于《周礼》，具体包括：

议亲：皇帝的亲属。

议故：皇帝的故交旧友。

议贤：德行高尚，其言论行动可作为法则者。

议能：能整顿军旅，治理内政，为皇帝出谋划策，师范人伦者。

议功：对朝廷尽忠效力，建立大功勋的人。

议贵：三品以上高级官员或有一品爵位的人。

议勤：高级文武官员中恪尽职守，专心致志办理公务的人。

议宾：前朝国君的后裔。

生词表

序号	生词	词性	汉语拼音	英文解释
1	八议	*proper n.*	Bā yì	leniency for eight privileged groups
2	贵族	*n.*	guì zú	nobility
3	法律特权	*phr.*	fǎ lǜ tè quán	legal privilege
4	八辟	*proper n.*	Bā Pì	the system prototype of "Bayi"
5	法典	*n.*	fǎ diǎn	code of laws
6	死刑	*n.*	sǐ xíng	capital punishment
7	审理	*v.*	shěn lǐ	adjudicate
8	奏请	*v.*	zòu qǐng	petition
9	裁决	*n.*	cái jué	decision，judgement
10	德行	*n.*	dé xíng	moral conduct
11	功勋	*n.*	gōng xūn	merits，distinguished services
12	亲属	*n.*	qīn shǔ	relatives
13	故交	*n.*	gù jiāo	old friends
14	师范	*n.*	shī fàn	role model
15	尽忠	*phr.*	jìn zhōng	serve loyally
16	专心致志	*idm.*	zhuān xīn zhì zhì	concentrate wholly on

重 点汉字【诉】

　　诉（sù），汉语一级字，本义指告状、控告。《说文解字》中解释为告知。《玉篇》中解释为论述或告诉冤枉的事情。《广韵》中解释为毁谤，如《左传·成公十六年》中记载，郤犫"诉公于晋侯"，此处对"诉"注解为"譖"，即诽谤。《史记·龟策列传》中记载，"王有德义，故来告诉"，其中"告诉"义为告知。"诉"原写作"愬"，在《论语》中，"肤受之愬"义为"像切肤之痛那样的诽谤"，"愬"即表诽谤之义；之后在《汉书·五行志》中将这个字引用为"诉"。此外，在《韵会小补》中"诉"字通作"遬"。《战国策》中记载，"卫君跣行，告遬于魏"，注解中说明"遬"和"愬"在这里都通"诉"字，表示告诉。

图 10-3　"诉"字篆刻（王琦　刻）

 汉字拓展

序号	词汇	汉语拼音	英文解释	例句
1	诉讼	sù sòng	lawsuit	他因为合同纠纷而提起了诉讼。
2	申诉	shēn sù	appeal	他对判决结果不满意，决定申诉。
3	投诉	tóu sù	complain	如果服务不满意，您可以向管理部门投诉。
4	告诉	gào sù	inform	请立即告诉我会议的具体时间。
5	诉求	sù qiú	demand, request	政府应该正视民众的诉求。
6	自诉	zì sù	prosecute oneself	在这种情况下，被告选择自诉。
7	诉讼费	sù sòng fèi	litigation costs	诉讼费将由败诉方承担。

续表

序号	词汇	拼音	英文解释	例句
8	陈诉	chén sù	narrate，recount	他向听众陈诉了自己的创业历程。
9	诉说	sù shuō	talk about	她喜欢在夜晚诉说自己的秘密。
10	冤诉	yuān sù	wrongful accusation	他为了自己的冤诉四处奔波。
11	控诉	kòng sù	accuse	她在法庭上控诉对方违反合同。

文 化知识【《千字文》】

　　《千字文》，原名《次韵王羲之书千字》，是南朝梁时期周兴嗣创作的一篇独特的韵文。这篇文作包含一千个不重复的汉字，起初是由梁武帝选取王羲之的一千个字样，用于其亲人练习书法。但字样排列杂乱，难以成篇，因此梁武帝命周兴嗣将这些字编排成文，以便于学习和记忆。《千字文》以其清晰的主题和连贯的结构著称，文中语言简洁而美观，辞藻华丽，充满了引经据典的文句，如《易经》《诗经》《尚书》《礼记》等，显示出深厚的文化底蕴。这篇文章不仅是一件展示儒家思想的作品，还融合了自然界、历史和社会的常识，结构严谨，意蕴深远。

图 10-4　陕西西安碑林：怀素草书千字文

作为一种重要的启蒙读物，《千字文》与《三字经》、《百家姓》、《千家诗》并称为"三百千千"，在古代中国的基础教育中占据重要地位。它不仅在中国广为流传，在整个汉字文化圈中都受到重视。历代以来，无数书法家都曾竞相书写《千字文》，其中包括智永、怀素、欧阳询、赵佶等大师，他们的作品至今仍被传颂。这些书法作品不仅是艺术珍品，也是汉字书写艺术的重要组成部分，展示了汉字的独特魅力和深远影响。

治文物【佉卢文买卖奴隶木牍】

图 10-5　汉晋北朝·佉卢文买卖奴隶木牍[1]

经典阅读

《千字文》（节选）

天地玄黄，宇宙洪荒。日月盈昃，辰宿列张。
寒来暑往，秋收冬藏。闰余成岁，律吕调阳。
云腾致雨，露结为霜。金生丽水，玉出昆冈。
剑号巨阙，珠称夜光。果珍李柰，菜重芥姜。
海咸河淡，鳞潜羽翔。龙师火帝，鸟官人皇。
始制文字，乃服衣裳。推位让国，有虞陶唐。
吊民伐罪，周发殷汤。坐朝问道，垂拱平章。

---

〔1〕　参见《汉晋北朝·佉卢文买卖奴隶木牍》，载中国政法大学中华法制文明虚拟博物馆，https://flgj.cupl.edu.cn/info/1091/1558.htm，最后访问日期：2024 年 9 月 27 日。

爱育黎首，臣伏戎羌。遐迩一体，率宾归王。

鸣凤在树，白驹食场。化被草木，赖及万方。

 参考译文

青黑色的天空，土黄色的大地，混沌之中诞生出宇宙。太阳升起又落下，月亮圆了又缺，星辰布陈于无边无际的太空。

寒冷与暑热循环往复；秋天收割庄稼，冬天储藏粮食。积累数年的闰日并成闰月、归于闰年；而六律和六吕可以用来进行阴阳调和。

水汽升腾形成雨，露水遇冷凝结成霜。黄金产自金沙江中，玉石出自昆仑山岗。

最锋利的宝剑叫"巨阙"，最贵重的明珠叫"夜光珠"。水果里最珍贵的是李子和柰子，蔬菜中最重要的是芥菜和生姜。

海水是咸的，河水是淡的，鱼儿在水中潜游，鸟儿在空中飞翔。被称为"龙师"的伏羲、被称为"火帝"的神农、被称为"鸟官"的少昊、还有人皇黄帝，他们都是上古时代的帝皇。

仓颉创制了文字，嫘祖制作了衣裳。唐尧、虞舜英明无私，主动把君位禅让给贤能之人。

周武王姬发和商王成汤安抚百姓、讨伐暴君；贤明的君主坐在朝廷上向大臣们询问治国之道，垂衣拱手之间，毫不费力就能使天下太平，功绩彰著。

他们体恤百姓，各族人民都俯首称臣。普天之下归于一统，所有的人都服从于贤德之君的统治。

凤凰在竹林中欢乐地鸣叫，小白马在草场上自由自在地吃着草。圣君贤王的仁德之治使草木都沾受了恩惠，恩泽遍及天下百姓。

The dark blue sky and the earth in yellow-brown hues gave birth to the universe amidst chaos. The sun rises and sets, the moon waxes and wanes, while stars scatter across the boundless sky.

The cold and the heat cycle continuously; in autumn crops are harvested, and in winter grains are stored. Extra days accumulated over the years form leap months and leap years, and the six tones and six pitches are used to balance yin and yang.

Water vapor ascends and forms rain, and dew condenses in the cold to become frost. Gold comes from the sands of the Jinsha River, and jade from the Kunlun Mountain.

The sharpest sword is called "Juque," and the most precious pearl is the "Nightlight Pearl." Among fruits, plums and apples are the finest, while mustard greens and ginger are the most important vegetables.

The seawater is salty, while river water is fresh; fish swim below the surface, and birds fly in the sky. The ancient emperors included Fuxi known as the "Dragon Master," Shennong known as the "Fire Emperor," Shaohao known as the "Bird Officer," and the Yellow Emperor known as "Emperor of mankind".

Cangjie created the written script, and Leizu invented clothing. Emperor Tang Yao and Emperor Yu Shun were wise and selfless, voluntarily passing the throne to the virtuous.

Jifa，known as the King Wu of Zhou and King Cheng Tang of Shang, pacified the people and overthrew tyrants; wise rulers sat in the court and consulted their ministers on governance, bringing peace to the realm with effortless gestures, and their achievements were remarkable.

They sympathized with the people, and all the tribes submitted in respect. Under their rule, the whole world was unified, and all people obeyed the virtuous ruler.

The phoenix joyfully sang among the bamboo groves, and the white horses grazed freely on the plains. The benevolent rule of the sage kings brought blessings even to the plants and trees, spreading grace across all the people of the land.

课 后练习

1. 选择题："八议"法律特权最初源自哪个时期？

A. 汉朝

B. 唐朝

C. 三国时期

D. 西周时期

2. 判断题：八议中的"议亲"指的是皇帝的近亲属享有特殊的法律地位。

3. 填空题：根据八议中的规定，若犯罪行将处流刑以下的刑罚，其刑罚可被直接_____。

4. 简答题：请解释"八议"中的"议贵"指的是哪一类人，并描述他们享有的特权内容。

5. 讨论题："八议"制度在维护封建社会秩序中的作用及其可能带来的社会影响。

课 文参考翻译

The concept of "Bayi" ("leniency for eight privileged groups") was a legal privilege enjoyed by ancient Chinese officials or nobles, originally stemming from the "Bapi" during the Western Zhou period. It was first codified in "New Laws" during the Three Kingdoms Period by Emperor Ming of Wei and has since been a fundamental institution in subsequent legal codes. The "Bayi" meant that judicial authorities could not directly handle capital offenses committed by those entitled to this privilege without first reporting the crime and the reasons for the privilege to the emperor, unless they've committed the "Ten Abominations". The emperor would then consult his ministers, and ultimately he would make a decision, usually exempting the individual from capital punishment. For crimes warranting penalties less severe than exile, the punishment could be directly reduced by one degree. However, this provision did not apply to those committing the "Ten Abominations."

The scope of the "Bayi" are detailed in *The Rites of Zhou*:

The deliberation of "亲 Qin": royal family members.

The deliberation of "故 Gu"：old acquaintances of the emperor.

The deliberation of "贤 Xian"：individuals of high moral standing whose actions and words could serve as standards.

The deliberation of "能 Neng"：those capable of organizing military forces and managing internal affairs to provide counsel to the emperor.

The deliberation of "功 Gong"：individuals who have demonstrated loyalty and made significant contributions to the court.

The deliberation of "贵 Gui"：high-ranking officials of the third rank and above or those holding the highest noble titles.

The deliberation of "勤 Qin"：high-ranking civil and military officials who diligently fulfill their duties.

The deliberation of "宾 Bin"：descendants of monarchs from previous dynasties.

第十一课

隋唐时期的法律（一）

图 11-1　中国国家博物馆：盛世修典——"中国历代绘画大系"成果展
隋·《游春图》（展子虔）

公元 581 年，掌握北周权力的外戚杨坚，逼迫北周静帝退位，建立隋朝。589 年隋南下灭陈，统一全国，结束了中国历史上长达三百多年的政治分裂局面。虽然隋朝仅存三十余年，但在政治、经济、文化、法律等各方面均有发展，对唐朝的影响不可忽视。特别是隋文帝时期的《开皇律》与隋炀帝时期的《大业律》。

隋朝统治后期，阶级矛盾和社会矛盾激化，各地的起义和反叛此起彼伏。公元 617 年，太原留守、唐国公李渊起兵，之后攻占长安（今西安）。618 年，隋炀帝被杀，李渊称帝，建立唐朝，改元武德。唐朝统治者在国家治理和社会管理方面，确立"德礼为政教之本，刑罚为政教之用"的基本原则，以儒家所倡导的"仁政""德治"为指导思想，进一步发展完善各项制度，使唐朝成为中国历史上的一个"盛世"时期。

In AD 581, Yang Jian, the influential relative by marriage of the Northern Zhou, forced Emperor Jing of Northern Zhou to abdicate and established the Sui Dynasty. In AD 589, Sui advanced southward to conquer the Chen

Dynasty, unifying the country and ending over 300 years of political fragmentation in Chinese history. Although the Sui Dynasty lasted only for about 30 years, it saw developments in politics, economy, culture, and law, and its impact on the subsequent Tang Dynasty was significant. Notably during the reign of Emperor Wen was the "Kaihuang Code," and during Emperor Yang's reign was the "Daye Code."

In the later period of Sui, class and social conflicts intensified, leading to various uprisings and rebellions across the regions. In AD 617, Li Yuan, the military governor of Taiyuan and Duke of Tang, rebelled and subsequently captured Chang'an (present-day Xi'an). In AD 618, after the assassination of Emperor Yang, Li Yuan proclaimed himself emperor, establishing the Tang Dynasty and marking the beginning with the Wude era. The rulers of the Tang Dynasty, guided by the Confucian ideals of "benevolent governance" and "rule by virtue," established the basic principles of governance where "virtue and rites formed the basis of government and education, while punishments served their enforcement." These principles further refined and perfected various systems, leading the Tang Dynasty to a period of great prosperity in Chinese history.

 生词表

序号	生词	词性	汉语拼音	英文解释
1	外戚	n.	wài qī	relatives by marriage（of the ruling family）
2	退位	v.	tuì wèi	abdicate
3	南下	phr.	nán xià	move or advance southward
4	统一	v.	tǒng yī	unify
5	分裂	n.	fēn liè	division，split
6	影响	n.	yǐng xiǎng	influence
7	激化	v.	jī huà	intensify

续表

序号	生词	词性	汉语拼音	英文解释
8	留守	*n.*	liú shǒu	a temporary military office
9	改元	*phr.*	gǎi yuán	change the era name
10	德礼	*phr.*	dé lǐ	virtue and etiquette
11	刑罚	*n.*	xíng fá	penalties，punishments
12	仁政	*n.*	rén zhèng	benevolent governance
13	德治	*n.*	dé zhì	rule by virtue
14	盛世	*n.*	shèng shì	golden age，period of prosperity

导 读

　　隋文帝杨坚认识到德礼在国家治理中的重要地位和作用，因此强调国家治理要以德礼为本，实现民众教化的重要方式是"以德代刑"。他在诏令中多次重申"礼"在国家治理中的重要意义。隋文帝同时意识到，制定法律要因时立法，有所沿革，不能完全照搬前代之法。此外，他还重视民风民俗，强调要尊重民间的风俗习惯。隋文帝在开皇元年诏令中也提出，要删减前代的严酷刑罚。不过，在施行仁政和德治的同时，隋朝的统治者也并未忽视法律和刑罚在治国理政、维持秩序方面的重要作用。但到了隋文帝统治后期和隋炀帝统治时期开始实施"轻罪重罚""严刑止奸"等刑事镇压措施，在很大程度上造成了社会混乱和一些冤假错案。沈家本在《历代刑法考》中对此评价道："观于炀帝之先轻刑而后淫刑，与文帝如出一辙。文淫刑而身被弑，炀淫刑而或遂亡。盖法善而不循法，法亦虚器而已。"[1]

课 文

　　隋朝建立之后，隋文帝在总结前代统治和治理经验的基础上，从政治、

---

　　〔1〕 参见朱勇主编：《中国法律史》，中国政法大学出版社 2021 年版，第 145~147 页。

经济、军事、法律等各个方面对皇权以及中央集权的制度进行了完善和维护。

图 11-2　中国国家博物馆：盛世修典——"中国历代绘画大系"成果展
唐·《历代帝王图（杨坚、杨广）》（阎立本）

　　隋文帝即位之初，就开始修订律令，在《北齐律》"重罪十条"的基础上，设置"十恶"的条款，同时规定了"八议""赎刑""官当"等内容。开皇三年，隋文帝"更定新律"，删减死刑、重刑等内容，最终完成《开皇律》的"更定"工作，共12卷、500条。《开皇律》确立起较为完善的十二篇的法典体例，在中国法律史上具有承上启下的重要意义，成为唐律制定的蓝本。《资治通鉴》对《开皇律》历史地位的评价是：**"自是法制遂定，后世多遵用之。"**

　　隋朝的法律形式主要有四种：律、令、格、式。虽然现今具体内容已经佚失，只能从一些文献典籍的记载中了解其零星的内容，但能够看出，隋朝已经确立起较为完善的律令格式法律体系，这体现出当时立法技术的进步和成熟。

　　与前代法律相比，隋朝在刑事法律方面也有不少发展和创新。《开皇律》以前代的五刑制为基础，确立了较为规范完备的新的五刑制：死刑、流刑、徒刑、杖刑、笞刑，并对这五种刑罚规定了相应的赎刑。例如，隋文帝开皇元年更定的赎刑中，"笞十者铜一斤……徒一年，赎铜二十斤……流一千里，赎铜八十斤……两千里则百斤矣"。隋炀帝制定的《大业律》增加了赎刑所需的铜数。根据《隋书·刑法志》记载，隋炀帝时期，徒期一年的赎铜60斤，每等级增加30斤；流刑赎铜240斤。[1]

 生词表

序号	生词	词性	汉语拼音	英文解释
1	治理	*n.*	zhì lǐ	administration
2	皇权	*n.*	huáng quán	imperial power
3	隋文帝	*proper n.*	Suí wén dì	Emperor Wen of Sui
4	即位	*v.*	jí wèi	ascend the throne
5	修订	*v.*	xiū dìng	revise
6	赎刑	*n.*	shú xíng	redemption of punishment
7	官当	*n.*	guān dāng	government post for punishment
8	删减	*v.*	shān jiǎn	cut down, reduce
9	蓝本	*n.*	lán běn	blueprint
10	格	*n.*	gé	regulations
11	佚失	*v.*	yì shī	lose
12	进步	*n.*	jìn bù	progress
13	创新	*n.*	chuàng xīn	innovation
14	规范	*n.*	guī fàn	norm, standard
15	完备	*adj.*	wán bèi	complete, comprehensive
16	赎	*v.*	shú	redeem
17	笞刑	*n.*	chī xíng	flogging punishment
18	杖刑	*n.*	zhàng xíng	punishment of beating
19	隋炀帝	*proper n.*	Suí yáng dì	Emperor Yang of Sui

---

〔1〕 参见朱勇主编：《中国法律史》，中国政法大学出版社2021年版，第147~151页。

续表

序号	生词	词性	汉语拼音	英文解释
20	大业律	*proper n.*	Dà yè Lǜ	Daye Code
21	隋书	*proper n.*	Suí Shū	Book of Sui
22	升级	*v.*	shēng jí	upgrade

重 点汉字【监】

　　"监"（jiān，jiàn），起源于商代甲骨文及金文。在古代字形中，它描述的是一个人弯腰低头朝向一个盛满水的容器，原始意义是使用水作为镜子来照看自己的倒影。由于这种照看是自上而下进行的，故逐渐衍生出从上向下监视的含义，进而发展成今天理解的监察、监督等词汇。早期，"监"也指用来照看自己影子的器物，这种用法在后世由"鉴"字承担。

图 11-3 "监"字篆刻（王琦 刻）

　　甲骨文中的"监"字形象为一个人在水容器中照看自己的面容，随着时代的推移，尤其是在战国时期，字形逐渐发生变化，人物与器皿中的水开始明显区分。到了小篆时期，人物和眼睛完全分离，使得原有的照面意义不再明显。而隶书将人物和水点都置于"皿"字的右上方，这一形式延续至楷书，并在唐代草书中简化为现在的"监"。

　　"监"字从其形象和功能的演变中，本义是照面或照影，指必须有盛水的容器。此字的应用也延伸至监视或观察，象征着严密的观察和审视，涉及道德、经验以及社会习俗的监察。如《诗经》中的"天监有周"展现了上天对周朝的监视。随时间推移，"监"不仅指实体的监视者或监察对象，还发展成为涵盖广泛的社会、政治和道德领域的抽象概念。

此外，"监"也用于形成多种复合词汇，如监视、监督、监察等，表明其在社会和政治中的广泛应用。职务上如监国、监抚等，机构上如监狱、国子监等，展示了"监"字在管理和教育中的重要角色。由实际的盛水容器到广义的监察概念，这一字的发展和应用，充分体现了语言的丰富性和适应性。

 ## 汉字拓展

序号	词汇	汉语拼音	英文解释	例句
1	监控	jiān kòng	monitor，surveillance	公司安装了监控系统以提高安全性。
2	监狱	jiān yù	prison	他被判入监狱服刑五年。
3	监督	jiān dū	supervise	他被任命去监督项目。
4	监管	jiān guǎn	regulation，oversight	银行业需要严格的监管以防止金融危机。
5	监测	jiān cè	monitor，measure	环保部门正在监测空气质量。
6	监视	jiān shì	observe，watch over	警察正在监视嫌疑人的一举一动。
7	监禁	jiān jìn	detain，confinement	他因涉嫌犯罪被监禁。
8	监护	jiān hù	guardianship	作为父亲，他对孩子有监护权。
9	监考	jiān kǎo	invigilate	教师需要监考以确保考试的公平。
10	监察	jiān chá	inspect	政府监察部门负责审查所有新提案。
11	监工	jiān gōng	overseer，foreman	监工负责确保工程按时完成。
12	监听	jiān tīng	eavesdrop	安全机构被授权对嫌疑人进行监听。
13	监押	jiān yā	escort under custody	警方监押犯人前往法庭。

文 化知识【颜氏家训】

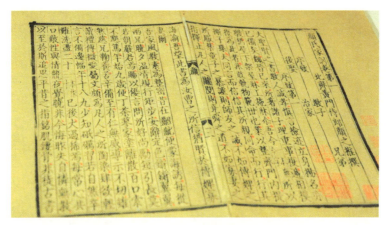

图 11-4　国家典籍博物馆：颜氏家训

《颜氏家训》是南北朝时期颜之推创作的家训。该书成书于隋文帝灭陈国以后，隋炀帝即位之前（约公元 6 世纪末）。是颜之推记述个人经历、思想、学识以告诫子孙的著作。

《颜氏家训》共有 7 卷，20 篇。颜之推不但日常深信因果、礼拜佛陀，还对奉佛及其所产生的问题形成了自己的一套观点，在《颜氏家训·归心》篇里，他对此作了充分论说。在颜之推看来，首先佛教高于儒教，儒学虽然知识渊深，教人仁、义、礼、智、信的修身之道，但不论从它知识的广博而言，还是就它所传导的从善内涵来说，它的精髓都已被包含在佛学之内，即佛教的知识和教义"明非尧舜、周孔所及也"。作为出身于世以儒学传承家族的士大夫，颜之推无法抹去儒家文化的浸润，所以在信仰佛教的同时又不能不受儒家思想的深刻影响。

颜之推并无赫赫之功，也未列显官之位，却因一部《颜氏家训》而享千秋盛名，由此可见其家训的影响深远。作为传统社会的典范教材，《颜氏家训》直接开后世"家训"的先河，是中国古代家庭教育理论宝库中的一份珍贵遗产。

法 治文物【县印】

图 11-4　隋·县印[1]

经 典阅读

《颜氏家训·音辞》（节选）

夫九州之人，言语不同，生民已来，固常然矣。自春秋标齐言之传，离骚目楚词之经，此盖其较明之初也。后有扬雄着方言，其言大备。然皆考名物之同异，不显声读之是非也。逮郑玄注六经，高诱解吕览、淮南，许慎造说文，刘熹制释名，始有譬况假借以证音字耳。而古语与今殊别，其间轻重清浊，犹未可晓；加以内言外言、急言徐言、读若之类，益使人疑。孙叔言创尔雅音义，是汉末人独知反语。至于魏世，此事大行。高贵乡公不解反语，

---

〔1〕参见《隋·县印》，载中国政法大学中华法制文明虚拟博物馆，https://flgj.cupl.edu.cn/info/1072/1739.htm，最后访问日期：2024 年 10 月 11 日。

以为怪异。自兹厥后，音韵锋出，各有土风，递相非笑，指马之谕，未知孰是。

 参考译文

九州之民的语言各不相同，这是自古以来的常态。自从《春秋》记载齐国的语言，到《离骚》被视为楚国诗歌的经典之作，这大概是古人明白各地语言存在差异的开始。后来，扬雄编写了《方言》，详细记载了各地的语言。然而，这些作品主要是记录名物的异同，并未明确阐述音韵的正确与否。直到郑玄注解六经，高诱注解《吕氏春秋》和《淮南子》，许慎撰写《说文解字》，刘熹制作《释名》，才开始用譬况法、假借法来为音同或音近的字注音。然而，古代和现代发音差别很大，其轻重清浊仍然不太清晰；加上他们注音的时候用的内言外言、急言徐言、读若之类的说法，更加增加了理解的困难。孙叔言创作了《尔雅音义》一书，是汉末唯一一个知道反切的人。到了魏代，用反切法注音变得非常普遍。若是高贵乡公不懂反切就会被认为很奇怪。从此以后，语音学开始发展，各地的方言各异，互相嘲笑，不知道哪种是正确的。

Since ancient times, the people of the Nine Provinces have spoken different languages; which has always been the case. The recording of Qi's speech in the *Spring and Autumn Annals* and the classic status of *Lisao* in Chu poetry marks the early beginnings of dialect documentation. Later, Yang Xiong composed the *Fangyan*, which extensively documented various regional languages. However, these works primarily focused on the similarities and differences in name of items, and did not clarify the correctness of pronunciations. It was not until Zheng Xuan annotated the Six Classics, Gao You interpreted *Master Lyv's Spring and Autumn Annals* and *Huai-nan-tzu*, Xu Shen created *Explaining and Analyzing Characters*, and Liu Xi produced *Shiming,* that people began to use analogies and hypotheticals with the same or similar pronunciation to demonstrate phonetics. However, the ancient pronunciation differed significantly from the modern, and the nuances of tones and sounds were still unclear.

Additionally, the expressions they used like "inner speech, outer speech, urgent speech, slow speech, mimic speech" added to the complexity of understanding. Sun Shuyan proclaimed *Erya Yinyi*, being the only one in the Han dynasty to know about Fanqie phonetics. By the Wei dynasty, this study had become widespread. The noble gentry misunderstood Fanqie phonetics, considered peculiar. Since then, the study of phonetics flourished, each region developed its own linguistic characteristics, and mutual mockery ensued over which dialect was correct.

课 后练习

1. 选择题：根据《开皇律》的赎刑制度，以下哪项刑罚的赎刑铜数最多？

A. 笞刑十下

B. 徒刑一年

C. 流刑一千里

D. 流刑两千里

2. 判断题：隋朝的法律形式只包括律和令。

3. 填空题：在隋文帝的赎刑制度中，徒刑一年的赎刑需要支付的铜数量是＿＿＿＿斤。

4. 简答题：描述隋文帝在《开皇律》中所做的法律改革有哪些显著特点？

5. 论述题：隋朝法律中"十恶"条款的设置对后世法律发展的影响。

课 文参考翻译

After the establishment of the Sui Dynasty, Emperor Wen of Sui, drawing from the governance experiences of his predecessors, refined and strengthened the imperial authority and centralization across political, economic, military, and legal dimensions.

Upon ascending the throne, Emperor Wen of Su: began to revise the laws, building upon the "Ten Abominable Offenses" from the "laws of the Northern Qi," setting forth new provisions such as the "Ten Abominations," as well as regulations on "Bayi," "redemption," "government post for punishment." In the third year of the Kaihuang era, he revised the laws, reducing the use of the death penalty and other severe punishments, and ultimately completed the newly revised "Kaihuang Code," comprising twelve volumes with five hundred articles. This code established a more comprehensive legal framework, forming a crucial link between past and future legal systems, and served as a blueprint for the Tang Code. *Zizhi Tongjian* remarked on the historical significance of the "Kaihuang Code": "From then on, the legal system was established, and later generations widely adhered to it."

The legal forms of the Sui Dynasty mainly included 律 statutes, 令 decrees, 格 regulations, and 式 protocols. Although the detailed contents have been lost to history, scattered information from various historical records shows that the Sui Dynasty had developed a more sophisticated system of laws, reflecting advances in legislative technique.

Compared to earlier laws, the Sui Dynasty's criminal laws also developed and innovated significantly. The "Kaihuang Code" built upon the prior five-penalty system, establishing a more standardized and comprehensive new system of five punishments: death penalty, exile, penal servitude, beating, and flogging, with specific redemption provisions set for these punishments. For instance, in the first year of the Kaihuang era, redemption for ten lashes was set at one jin of copper; one year of penal servitude could be redeemed for twenty jin of copper; one thousand miles of exile for eighty jin, and two thousand miles for one hundred jin. Under Emperor Yang of Sui, the "Daye Code" increased the amount of copper required for redemption. According to *The Book of Sui: Penal Laws*, during Emperor Yang's reign, one year of penal servitude could be redeemed for sixty jin of copper, with each additional degree of punishment requiring thirty more jin; and redemption for exile could require up to two hundred and forty jin of copper.

第十二课

隋唐时期的法律（二）

图 12-1　陕西历史博物馆：唐仕女陶俑

　　唐朝初期，统治者从隋朝的灭亡中吸取了深刻的教训，并以儒家的正统思想为指南，开展了一系列的立法活动。唐朝的立法工作主要集中在唐代前中期，特别是在唐高祖武德年间、唐太宗贞观年间、唐高宗永徽年间以及唐玄宗开元年间。

　　唐初的统治思想强调"德礼为政教之本，刑罚为政教之用"，这表明唐初的统治者秉承仁政，即统治者应"爱民厚俗"，通过仁慈宽厚的政策治理天下，同时在刑罚应用上更为谨慎。唐初著名的政治家魏徵曾经上奏称，真正的圣明君主应该通过推广仁义来改变风俗，而不是依赖严苛的法律和刑罚。

因此，唐太宗总结历史经验，明白了只有通过仁义来治国，国家才能长期稳定。

鉴于隋炀帝时期的严苛政策导致人民痛苦，唐高祖李渊起兵时就发布了"宽大之令"，登基后，他废除了隋朝繁复严苛的法律，并制定了更为宽简的法律。他还特别强调法令应当符合时宜，简洁明了，便于施行。唐太宗李世民在治国时也强调法律的简约性，反对法律格式过于烦琐，认为这会使官员难以掌握，容易滋生欺诈。

因此，唐朝的法律制定旨在反映国家和社会的实际需求，法律内容注重实用和简洁，刑罚趋于轻缓。唐太宗时期，他在修改法律时提出以宽简为基本原则，根据具体情况适当调整刑罚的重轻，大幅减少了死刑和肉刑的使用，体现了他对生命的珍视和对刑罚的慎用。

这种以"宽简"为核心，结合"据礼论情"的立法原则，不仅仅体现在刑罚的轻缓上，也意味着法律的公平和适中。唐太宗之后，唐高宗时期的长孙无忌等人也提到了法律应当"宽平适中"的原则，这种思想为唐朝后期乃至更远的历史时期提供了重要的法治思想和实践经验。[1]

In the early Tang Dynasty, rulers drew profound lessons from the collapse of the Sui Dynasty and initiated a series of legislative activities guided by Confucian orthodox ideology. The main legislative efforts in the Tang Dynasty were concentrated in the early to mid-Tang period, especially during the reigns of Emperor Gaozu in the Wude era, Emperor Taizong in the Zhenguan era, Emperor Gaozong in the Yonghui era, and Emperor Xuanzong in the Kaiyuan era.

The ruling philosophy of the early Tang emphasized "virtue and rites formed the basis of government and education, while punishment served their enforcement," indicating that early Tang rulers adhered to benevolent governance. They believed that rulers should "love the people and enrich cus-

---

〔1〕　参见朱勇主编：《中国法律史》，中国政法大学出版社 2021 年版，第 158~160 页。

toms" through compassionate and generous policies while applying criminal law more prudently. The renowned political advisor Wei Zheng once advised that a truly sage monarch should change customs through the promotion of benevolence and righteousness rather than relying on harsh laws and punishments. Thus, Emperor Taizong of Tang, learning from history, understood that the country could only be stable long-term through governance based on benevolence and righteousness.

Given the harsh policies during the reign of Emperor Yang of Sui that led to public suffering, Emperor Gaozu of Tang issued orders of leniency when he raised his army. Upon ascending the throne, he abolished the complicated and harsh laws of the Sui Dynasty and enacted simpler, more lenient laws. He also emphasized that laws should be appropriate to the times, straightforward, and easy to implement. Emperor Taizong of Tang also stressed the simplicity of laws during his reign, opposing overly complicated legal formats, which he believed made it difficult for officials to master and could foster deceit.

Therefore, the legal formulations of the Tang Dynasty aimed to reflect the actual needs of the state and society, with laws focusing on practicality and simplicity, and penalties tending to be more lenient. During Emperor Taizong's era, he advocated for simplicity as a fundamental principle in revising laws, adjusting the severity of penalties according to specific circumstances, and significantly reduced the use of capital and corporal punishment, reflecting his respect for life and cautious use of penal sanctions.

This principle of "leniency and simplicity," combined with the legislative principle of "according to propriety and discussing circumstances," was not only reflected in the moderation of punishments but also implied fairness and moderation in law. After Emperor Taizong, figures like Chancellor Zhangsun Wuji during Emperor Gaozong's reign also mentioned the principle that laws should be "lenient, fair, and moderate." This ideology provided significant legal and practical experience for later periods in Tang history and beyond.

生词表

序号	生词	词性	汉语拼音	英文解释
1	统治者	*n.*	tǒng zhì zhě	ruler
2	灭亡	*v.*	miè wáng	perish，be annihilated
3	谨慎	*adj.*	jǐn shèn	cautious，prudent
4	繁复	*adj.*	fán fù	complicated，complex
5	废除	*v.*	fèi chú	abolish，repeal
6	格式	*n.*	gé shì	format，style
7	简约	*adj.*	jiǎn yuē	simple and concise
8	法令	*n.*	fǎ lìng	laws and decrees
9	烦琐	*adj.*	fán suǒ	cumbersome，tedious
10	实用	*adj.*	shí yòng	practical，pragmatic
11	轻缓	*adj.*	qīng huǎn	lenient，mild
12	宽松	*adj.*	kuān sōng	relaxed，loose
13	法治思想	*phr.*	fǎ zhì sī xiǎng	legal philosophy
14	实践经验	*phr.*	shí jiàn jīng yàn	practical experience

导 读

自西汉武帝时期"罢黜百家，独尊儒术"以后，儒家思想逐渐成为正统统治思想而受到重视。经过魏晋南北朝时期的"法律儒家化"发展，从隋朝起，儒家思想已经正式成为立法的指导思想。

在西汉董仲舒阐述的"德主刑辅"思想的基础上，唐朝将"礼"的精神原则融入律典规定之中，确立起**"德礼为政教之本，刑罚为政教之用"**的思想原则并以之作为立法和执法的指导思想。

基础法律汉语（上册）

课 文

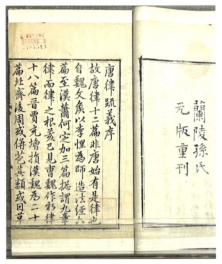

图 12-2　中国考古博物馆：唐·《唐律疏议》清刻本

《唐律疏议·名例》载："**德礼为政教之本，刑罚为政教之用，犹昏晓阳秋，相须而成者也。**""德礼"和"刑罚"就像昼夜更替、春去秋来一样同为治理国家所必需，二者缺一不可。这揭示出礼与法、德与刑在国家治理中的作用关系，突出了德礼在政教中的本体地位，明确刑罚在政教中的辅助作用。德礼重在教化劝导，劝民以礼，导民向善，而刑罚的作用重在禁顽止奸，惩罚犯罪。二者功能互补，相辅相成。

《唐律疏议》的体例和内容以隋朝的《开皇律》及此前的《武德律》《贞观律》为蓝本，共 12 篇，500 条。十二篇分别为《名例》《卫禁》《职制》《户婚》《厩库》《擅兴》《贼盗》《斗讼》《诈伪》《杂律》《捕亡》《断狱》。《名例》位于律首，相当于现代的"总则"，其中规定刑罚的种类及其适用规定、定罪量刑的一般性规定等内容。疏议曰："**名者，五刑之罪名；例者，五刑之体例……命诸篇之刑名，比诸篇之法例。**"最后两篇《捕亡》和《断狱》的内容多为程序性规定，其余各篇的规定基本是各种具体犯罪及相应刑罚的内容。依此，《唐律疏议》所确立的是"总则—实体法—程序法"的基本结构。从另一个方面看，《卫禁》《职制》《户婚》《厩库》《擅兴》五篇可归为"事律"，《贼盗》《斗讼》《诈伪》《杂律》《捕亡》五篇可归为"罪律"，《断狱》篇可视为"专则"。据此，《唐律疏议》的基本结构亦可看作"始以总则，终以专则，先列事律，后列罪律"，反映出唐律在立法技术上的成熟。[1]

 生词表

序号	生词	词性	汉语拼音	英文解释
1	昏晓	*phr.*	hūn xiǎo	dawn and dusk
2	阳秋	*phr.*	yáng qiū	spring and autumn
3	缺一不可	*idm.*	quē yī bù kě	indispensable, essential
4	教化	*n.*	jiào huà	education and transformation
5	劝导	*v.*	quàn dǎo	guide, advise
6	导民	*v.*	dǎo mín	lead the people
7	向善	*v.*	xiàng shàn	turn to goodness
8	禁顽	*phr.*	jìn wán	prohibit lawbreaker
9	止奸	*phr.*	zhǐ jiān	stop treachery
10	功能	*n.*	gōng néng	function, capability
11	互补	*adj.*	hù bǔ	complementary
12	厩库	*proper n.*	Jiù kù	law about stables and storehouses
13	擅兴	*proper n.*	Shàn xīng	law about act without permission
14	斗讼	*proper n.*	Dòu sòng	law about claim for affray
15	诈伪	*proper n.*	Zhà wěi	law about fraud and deceit
16	杂律	*proper n.*	Zá lù	miscellaneous laws
17	事律	*n.*	shì lù	laws regarding affairs
18	罪律	*n.*	zuì lù	criminal laws

---

〔1〕 参见朱勇主编：《中国法律史》，中国政法大学出版社 2021 年版，第 158~162 页。

点汉字【告】

　　"告"（gào），最早出现在商朝的甲骨文中。其基本含义是进行祭祀。随着时间的推移，"告"字的含义逐渐丰富，扩展到大声宣布、表达、请求、辞别以及向公众通知等多重意义。甲骨文中的"告"字形象中，上部分象征牛头，下部分则是盛放牛头的容器，反映出古代用牛进行祭祀的场景。金文和篆体的字形保持了与甲骨文相似的结构。"告"字是一个典型的会意字，上部的"牛"代表用于祭祀的牲畜，下部的"口"则暗示诉说或祝祷的行为。在古代，牛是高规格的祭祀用牲畜，通常仅在重大的仪式中使用。牛口中诉说祈祷的言语，字义扩展到了"告诉"。这个词义进一步扩展到了公告、教育、上报、告状和请求等，如"告示""谕告"指明公开通知或指示，"上告"或"上报"包含向上级报告的意思，"告状"和"揭发"则有法律和申诉方面的意义，并从"请求"进一步衍生出休假等具体行为的表达。从祭祀的原始意义到复杂的社会交流功能的演变过程，展示了汉字"告"的文化深度。

图 12-3　"告"字篆刻（王琦 刻）

◆ 汉字拓展

序号	词汇	汉语拼音	英文解释	例句
1	告诉	gào sù	tell, inform	请告诉我你的决定。
2	报告	bào gào	report, inform	他正在准备明天的会议报告。

续表

序号	词汇	汉语拼音	英文解释	例句
3	告别	gào bié	say goodbye	明天我们将举行一个简单的告别仪式。
4	告发	gào fā	denounce，accuse	他决定告发那些违法的同事。
5	告急	gào jí	emergency，distress	由于食物短缺，村庄向政府告急。
6	申告	shēn gào	declare，report	今年的所得税申告截止日期已经临近。
7	控告	kòng gào	accuse，sue	他决定控告对方违约。
8	告状	gào zhuàng	sue，complain	她不得不向警方告状。
9	警告	jǐng gào	warn，caution	教师给出了一个严重的警告。
10	判告	pàn gào	inform by judgement	法官将判告被告的罪名。
11	告示	gào shì	show and tell	老师张贴告示对项目进行说明。
12	告终	gào zhōng	end，conclude	仪式以简短的演讲告终。
13	告捷	gào jié	report a victory	战场上的将军通过信号灯向总部告捷。
14	告白	gào bái	confess，profess	电影中的主角在雨中向他的爱人告白。

文 化知识【"三法司"】

　　夏商时期，判决案件由"獬豸"进行神判，西周开始设"司寇"行使司法权。战国时期的秦国，设立"御史"以维护法纪；秦始皇统一中国后，除了"御史"以外，又设置了处理普通案件的"廷尉"，由此形成了秦朝的"二法司"。西汉的汉成帝开始设立"三公尚书"，逐渐形成"三法司"制度：廷尉负责案件初审，复审的权限由三公尚书执掌，御史台依然负责特殊案件。特别需要提及的一个名称是"诏狱"，它主要关押的是皇帝交办的特殊案件中的贵族和官员。魏晋南北朝时期，"廷尉"改名为"大理寺"。至唐朝，"刑部尚书"取代"三公尚书"。从此，中国历史上的"三法司"制度和名称正式确立，"三法司"包括大理寺、刑部和御史台。大理寺为初级审判机关；刑部是中央复审机关；御史台负责监察、刑法典章和官员犯罪，是特别审判机构。

图 12-4　河南博物院：武则天金简

　治文物【月宫镜】

图 12-5　唐·月宫镜[1]

---

〔1〕参见《唐·月宫镜》，载中国政法大学中华法制文明虚拟博物馆，https://flgj.cupl.edu.cn/info/1072/4055.htm，最后访问日期：2024 年 9 月 27 日。

典阅读

《太平广记》卷第一百二十一报应二十冤报（节选）

唐秋官侍郎周兴与来俊臣对推事。俊臣别奉进止鞫兴，兴不之知也。及同食，谓兴曰："囚多不肯承，若为作法？"兴曰："甚易也。取大瓮，以炭四面炙之，令囚人处之其中，何事不吐？"即索大瓮，以火围之，起谓兴曰："有内状勘老兄，请兄入此瓮。"兴惶恐叩头，咸即款伏。

◆ 参考译文

唐代的周兴和来俊臣都是司职审判的酷吏。一日，来俊臣奉旨严查周兴，周兴对此并不知情。来俊臣把周兴请到自己家里吃饭，来俊臣对周兴说："兄弟我平日办案，常遇到一些犯人死不认罪，不知老兄有何办法？"周兴说："这还不好办！你找一个大瓮，四周用炭火烤热，再让犯人进到瓮里，你想想，还有什么事不招供呢？"来俊臣随即命人抬来一口大瓮，按周兴说的那样，在四周点上炭火，然后回头对周兴说："宫里有人密告你谋反，上边命我严查。对不起，现在就请老兄自己钻进瓮里吧。"周兴一听，扑通一声跪倒在地，连连磕头认罪。[1]

Zhou Xing and Lai Junchen in the Tang Dynasty were both cruel officials in charge of official trials. One day, Lai Junchen served strict inspection on Zhou Xing, Zhou Xing did not know. Lai Junchen prepared a lavish banquet and invited Zhou

---

〔1〕唐朝女皇武则天统治时期，为了镇压反对她的人，任用了一批酷吏。其中有两个最为狠毒，一个叫周兴，一个叫来俊臣。他们利用诬陷、控告和惨无人道的刑罚，杀害了许多正直的文武官吏和平民百姓。有一回，一封告密信送到武则天手里，内容是告发周兴与人联络谋反。武则天大怒，责令来俊臣严查此事。来俊臣苦苦思索半天，终于想出一条妙计，这一故事后来被称为"请君入瓮"，指以其人之法、还治其人之身。参见经典课程编委会编著：《北大历史课》，北京联合出版公司 2014 年版，第 97 页。

Xing to his home, and said to Zhou Xing, "Brother, when I handle cases, I often encounter criminals who stubbornly refuse to confess. Do you have any methods to share?" Zhou Xing replied, "That's easy! Get a large vat, heat it with charcoal all around, and then put the criminal inside. Think about it, who wouldn't confess then?" Lai Junchen then ordered his men to bring a large vat and set it up as Zhou had described, with charcoal fires lit around it. He then turned to Zhou Xing and said, "Someone in the palace secretly reported that you are plotting a rebellion. The order from above is to investigate rigorously. I'm sorry, but please enter the vat yourself." Hearing this, Zhou Xing immediately knelt down, repeatedly kowtowing and admitted his guilt.

课 后练习

1. 选择题：《唐律疏议》中的"名例"章节在律书中的作用类似于现代法律中的哪一个部分？

A. 实体法

B. 程序法

C. 总则

D. 附则

2. 判断题：《唐律疏议》是唐朝独有的法律形式，之前的朝代未有此类编纂。

3. 填空题：《唐律疏议》的编纂使用了_____和_____等律书作为蓝本。

4. 简答题：《唐律疏议》中的"捕亡"和"断狱"两章主要涉及哪些内容？

5. 论述题：《唐律疏议》中"德礼"与"刑罚"如何体现出互补和相辅相成的关系，并说明这种关系在国家治理中的意义。

课 文参考翻译

"Commentary on Law Codes of Tang Dynasty：Names and Examples" states: "Virtue and rites formed the basis of government and education, while punishments served their enforcement，as necessary to each other as day is to night, and spring is to autumn." Both "virtue and rites" and "punishments" are indispensable for governing the country. This highlights the relationship between rites and law, virtue and punishment in national governance, emphasizing the fundamental role of virtue and rites in governance and education, and clarifying the supportive role of penalties. Virtue and rites focus on educating and guiding the people, persuading them towards goodness, while penal sanctions primarily prevent lawbreaker and punish crimes. The two functions complement and support each other.

The structure and content of "Commentary on Law Codes of Tang Dynasty" are based on the "Kaihuang Code" of the Sui Dynasty, and earlier codes like the "Wude Code" and the "Zhenguan Code"，comprising twelve chapters and five hundred statutes. These chapters include "Names and Examples," "Guard and Prohibition," "Official Systems," "Family and Marriage," "Stables and Storehouses," "Unauthorized Construction," "Laws on Theft," "Laws on injury," "Laws on Fraud," "Miscellaneous Laws," "Pursuit of Escapees," and "Legal Adjudication." "Names and Examples," situated at the beginning of the code, functions similarly to the "General Provisions" in modern law, outlining the types of penalties and their application, along with general regulations for sentencing and defining crimes. The commentary notes, "The term '名' refers to the names of the five penalties；'例' refers to the model for these penalties...issuing the penal names through the chapters, comparing the legal examples." The last two chapters, "Pursuit of Escapees" and "Legal Adjudication," mostly contain procedural regulations, while the others detail specific crimes and their corresponding punishments.

Thus, "Commentary on Law Codes of Tang Dynasty " establishes a basic structure of "General Provisions—Substantive Law—Procedural Law." Look at it another way, chapters such as "Guard and Prohibition," "Official Systems," "'Family and Marriage," "Stables and Storehouses," "Unauthorized Construction," can be categorized as "regulatory laws," while "Laws on Theft," "Laws on injury," "Laws on Fraud," "Miscellaneous Laws," "Pursuit of Escapees," can be categorized as "penal laws." "Legal Adjudication," as a "special provision." This structure, starting with general provisions and ending with special provision, listing regulatory laws first followed by penal laws, reflects the maturity of Tang legislative techniques.

唐律疏议 卷第一 名例 *

* （唐）长孙无忌等撰：《唐律疏议》，刘俊文点校，中华书局 1983 年版，第 1~3 页。

【疏】議曰：夫三才肇位，萬象斯分。禀氣含靈，人爲稱首。莫不憑黎元而樹司宰，因政教而施刑法。其有情恣庸愚，識沈愆戾，大則亂其區宇，小則睽其品式，不立制度，則未之前聞。故曰：「以刑止刑，以殺止殺。」刑罰不可弛於國，笞捶不得廢於家。時遇澆淳，用有衆寡。於是結繩啟路，盈坎疏源，輕刑明威，大禮崇敬。易曰：「天垂象，聖人則之。」觀雷電而制威刑，睹秋霜而有肅殺，懲其未犯而防其未然，平其徽纆而存乎博愛，蓋聖王不獲已而用之。古者大刑用甲兵，其次用斧鉞；中刑用刀鋸，其次用鑽笮；薄刑用鞭扑。其所由來，亦已尚矣！昔白龍、白雲，則伏犧、軒轅之代；西火、西水，則炎帝、共工之年。鷦鳩筮賓於少皞，金政策名於顓頊。咸有天秩，典司刑憲。大道之化，擊壤無違。逮乎唐虞，化行事簡，議刑以定其罪，畫象以媿其心，所有條貫，良多簡略，年代浸遠，不可得而詳焉。堯舜時，理官則謂之爲「士」，而皋陶爲之；其法略存，而往往概見，則風俗通所云「皋陶謨：虞造律」是也。律者，訓銓，訓法也。易曰：「理財正辭，禁人爲非曰義。」故銓量輕重，依義制律。尚書大傳曰：「丕天之大律。」注云：「奉天之大法。」法亦律也，故謂之爲律。昔者，聖人制作謂之爲經，傳師所說則謂之爲傳，此則丘明、子夏於春秋、禮經作傳是也。近代以來，兼經注而明之則謂之爲義疏。疏之爲字，本以疏闊、疏遠立名。又，廣雅云：「疏者，識也。」案疏訓識，則書疏記識之道存焉。史記云：「前主所是著爲律，後主所是疏爲令。」漢書云：「削牘爲疏。」故云疏也。

昔者，三王始用肉刑。赭衣難嗣，皇風更遠，樸散淳離，傷肌犯骨。《尚書大傳》曰：「夏刑三千條。」《周禮》「司刑掌五刑」，其屬二千五百。穆王度時制法，五刑之屬三千。周衰刑重，戰國異制，魏文侯師於里悝，集諸國刑典，造《法經》六篇：一、《盜法》；二、《賊法》；三、《囚法》；四、《捕法》；五、《雜法》；六、《具法》。商鞅傳授，改法爲律。漢相蕭何，更加悝所造《戶》、《興》、《廄》三篇，謂《九章之律》。魏因漢律爲一十八篇，改漢《具律》爲《刑名第一》。晉命賈充等，增損漢、魏律爲二十篇，於魏《刑名律》中分爲《法例律》。宋齊梁及後魏，因而不改。爰至北齊，併《刑名》、《法例》爲《名例》。後周復爲《刑名》。隋因北齊，更爲《名例》。唐因於隋，相承不改。

名者，五刑之罪名；例者，五刑之體例。名訓爲命，例訓爲比，命諸篇之刑
名，比諸篇之法例。但名因罪立，事由犯生，命名即刑應，比例即事表，故
以《名例》爲首篇。第者，訓居，訓次，則次第之義，可得言矣。一者，太
極之氣，函三爲一，黃鍾之一，數所生焉。《名例》冠十二篇之首，故云「《名
例第一》」。大唐皇帝以上聖凝圖，英聲嗣武，潤春雲於品物，緩秋官於黎庶。
今之典憲，前聖規模，章程靡失，鴻纖備舉，而刑憲之司執行殊異：大理當
其死坐，刑部處以流刑；一州斷以徒年，一縣將爲杖罰。不有解釋，觸塗睽
誤。皇帝彝憲在懷，納隍興軫。德禮爲政教之本，刑罰爲政教之用，猶昏曉
陽秋相須而成者也。是以降綸言於台鉉，揮折簡於髦彦，爰造《律疏》，大明
典式。遠則皇王妙旨，近則蕭、賈遺文，沿波討源，自枝窮葉，甄表寬大，
裁成簡久。譬權衡之知輕重，若規矩之得方圓。邁彼三章，同符畫一者矣。

索引一

课文生词表汇总

序号	生词	词性	汉语拼音	英文解释	所在课文
1	八辟	*proper n.*	Bā pì	the system prototype of "Bayi"	10
2	八议	*proper n.*	Bā yì	leniency for eight privileged groups	10
3	崩溃	*v.*	bēng kuì	collapse	5
4	避舍	*v.*	bì shè	take shelter	4
5	边让	*proper n.*	Biān Ràng	a person's name	8
6	鞭刑	*n.*	biān xíng	whipping punishment	3
7	秉承	*v.*	bǐng chéng	uphold, inherit	2
8	卜辞	*n.*	bǔ cí	divination text	2
9	部落联盟	*n.*	bù luò lián méng	tribal alliance	1
10	不享	*phr.*	bù xiǎng	not to submit	1
11	裁决	*n.*	cái jué	decision, judgement	10
12	残酷	*adj.*	cán kù	cruel	6
13	沉迷	*v.*	chén mí	indulge	6
14	臣子	*n.*	chén zǐ	subject, minister	4
15	惩罚	*v.*	chéng fá	punish	8
16	惩戒	*n.*	chéng jiè	punishment, disciplinary action	2
17	笞刑	*n.*	chī xíng	flogging punishment	11
18	持续性	*n.*	chí xù xìng	continuity, persistence	9
19	初心	*n.*	chū xīn	original intention, aspiration	6
20	处决	*v.*	chǔ jué	execute	4
21	储主	*n.*	chǔ zhǔ	crown prince, heir apparent	4
22	传播	*v.*	chuán bō	spread, disseminate	9
23	创新	*n.*	chuàng xīn	innovation	11
24	春秋	*proper n.*	Chūn qiū	a book's name	8
25	刺字	*phr.*	cì zì	tattoo the face	1

续表

序号	生词	词性	汉语拼音	英文解释	所在课文
26	错误地	*adv.*	cuò wù de	erroneously	6
27	大忌	*n.*	dà jì	taboo	9
28	大辟	*n.*	dà pì	death penalty	3
29	大业律	*proper n.*	Dà yè Lǜ	Daye Code	11
30	大宗	*n.*	dà zōng	main branch of a family	3
31	怠慢	*v.*	dài màn	neglect，disregard	8
32	导民	*v.*	dǎo mín	lead the people	12
33	德	*n.*	dé	virtue，morality	3
34	德行	*n.*	dé xíng	moral conduct	10
35	德主刑辅	*idm.*	dé zhǔ xíng fǔ	virtue leads and punishment supports	3
36	地处	*v.*	dì chù	locate	5
37	典范	*n.*	diǎn fàn	model，example	6
38	斗讼	*proper n.*	Dòu sòng	law about claim for affray	12
39	动荡不安	*adj.*	dòng dàng bù ān	unstable，turbulent	6
40	独尊法家	*phr.*	dú zūn fǎ jiā	exclusively honor the Legalist school	5
41	法典	*n.*	fǎ diǎn	code of laws	10
42	法家	*proper n.*	Fǎ jiā	Legalism，school of thought in Chinese philosophy	5
43	法律特权	*phr.*	fǎ lǜ tè quán	legal privilege	10
44	繁法酷刑	*phr.*	fán fǎ kù xíng	overly harsh laws and cruel punishments	5
45	刖	*n.*	fèi	foot amputation punishment	3
46	封建	*n.*	fēng jiàn	feudalism	9
47	服丧	*phr.*	fú sāng	be in mourning	7
48	父权	*n.*	fù quán	paternal authority	9

续表

序号	生词	词性	汉语拼音	英文解释	所在课文
49	复杂	*adj.*	fù zá	complex	1
50	概念	*n.*	gài niàn	concept	9
51	干戈	*n.*	gān gē	arms，warfare	1
52	割鼻	*phr.*	gē bí	cut off the nose	1
53	割耳	*phr.*	gē ěr	cut off the ears	1
54	格	*n.*	gé	regulations	11
55	宫	*n.*	gōng	castration punishment	3
56	功能	*n.*	gōng néng	function，capability	12
57	宫室	*n.*	gōng shì	palace rooms	7
58	宫廷管理者	*n.*	gōng tíng guǎn lǐ zhě	court administrator	4
59	故交	*n.*	gù jiāo	old friends	10
60	寡人	*n.*	guǎ rén	I（self-reference by ancient kings）	5
61	官当	*n.*	guān dāng	government post for punishment	11
62	官职体系	*phr.*	guān zhí tǐ xì	official system	1
63	规范	*n.*	guī fàn	norm，standard	11
64	贵族	*n.*	guì zú	nobility	10
65	合法性	*n.*	hé fǎ xìng	legitimacy	2
66	洪水灾害	*n.*	hóng shuǐ zāi hài	flood disaster	1
67	后门	*n.*	hòu mén	back door	4
68	互补	*adj.*	hù bǔ	complementary	12
69	华丽	*adj.*	huá lì	gorgeous，splendid	7
70	画策	*n.*	huà cè	strategy，policy	1
71	桓邵	*proper n.*	Huán Shào	a person's name	8

续表

序号	生词	词性	汉语拼音	英文解释	所在课文
72	皇权	*n.*	huáng quán	imperial power	11
73	诙谐	*adj.*	huī xié	humorous	8
74	昏晓	*phr.*	hūn xiǎo	dawn and dusk	12
75	混乱	*n.*	hùn luàn	chaos	6
76	积水	*n.*	jī shuǐ	accumulated water，puddle	4
77	疾苦	*n.*	jí kǔ	suffering，hardship	6
78	即位	*v.*	jí wèi	ascend the throne	11
79	祭祀	*v.*	jì sì	offer sacrifices to gods	7
80	嘉石	*n.*	jiā shí	a form of punishment or labor	3
81	监察官	*n.*	jiān chá guān	inspector	1
82	奸臣	*n.*	jiān chén	treacherous official	6
83	肩胛骨	*n.*	jiān jiǎ gǔ	scapula，shoulder blade	2
84	简化	*v.*	jiǎn huà	simplify	7
85	教化	*n.*	jiào huà	education and transformation	12
86	借故	*phr.*	jiè gù	find some excuse	8
87	巾囊	*n.*	jīn náng	small pouch	8
88	进步	*n.*	jìn bù	progress	11
89	禁顽	*phr.*	jìn wán	prohibit lawbreaker	12
90	尽忠	*phr.*	jìn zhōng	serve loyally	10
91	经济基础	*n.*	jīng jì jī chǔ	economic base	5
92	荆庄王	*proper n.*	Jīng zhuāng wáng	King Zhuang of Jing	4
93	敬畏	*v.*	jìng wèi	revere，awe	2
94	九州	*proper n.*	Jiǔ zhōu	Nine Provinces of ancient China	1
95	厩库	*proper n.*	Jiù kù	law about stables and storehouses	12

续表

序号	生词	词性	汉语拼音	英文解释	所在课文
96	举殳	*phr.*	jǔ shū	raise a weapon	4
97	爵位	*n.*	jué wèi	noble rank	4
98	君臣	*phr.*	jūn chén	ruler and minister	7
99	钧金	*n.*	jūn jīn	thirty jin of metal，metaphor for legal fee	3
100	郡守	*n.*	jùn shǒu	prefect	5
101	开创性	*n.*	kāi chuàng xìng	pioneering，innovation	9
102	苛刻	*adj.*	kē kè	harsh，stringent	6
103	宽赦	*v.*	kuān shè	amnesty	9
104	蓝本	*n.*	lán běn	blueprint	11
105	燎祭	*n.*	liáo jì	burning sacrifice	2
106	凌驾	*v.*	líng jià	override	4
107	囹圄成市	*idm.*	líng yǔ chéng shì	prisons as crowded as markets	5
108	流刑	*n.*	liú xíng	exile punishment	3
109	露宿	*v.*	lù sù	sleep outdoors	4
110	马蹄	*n.*	mǎ tí	horse's hoof	4
111	麦田	*n.*	mài tián	wheat field	8
112	茅门之法	*proper n.*	Máo mén zhī fǎ	a law to guarantee the safety of the king	4
113	灭族	*v.*	miè zú	exterminate one's family/clan	8
114	墨	*n.*	mò	tattooing punishment	3
115	谋略	*n.*	móu luè	strategy，tactics	8
116	谋士	*n.*	móu shì	strategist，counselor	6
117	内部事务	*phr.*	nèi bù shì wù	internal affairs	1
118	配天	*phr.*	pèi tiān	match heaven	3
119	偏僻	*adj.*	piān pì	remote，secluded	5

序号	生词	词性	汉语拼音	英文解释	所在课文
120	平土	*n.*	píng tǔ	leveling land	1
121	起义军	*n.*	qǐ yì jūn	rebel army	6
122	器皿	*n.*	qì mǐn	utensils，vessels	7
123	契约	*n.*	qì yuē	contract	3
124	强制性	*adj.*	qiáng zhì xìng	compulsory	1
125	亲密关系	*n.*	qīn mì guān xì	close relationship	7
126	亲亲	*phr.*	qīn qīn	favor relatives	3
127	亲属	*n.*	qīn shǔ	relatives	10
128	轻佻	*adj.*	qīng tiāo	frivolous	8
129	请死罪	*phr.*	qǐng sǐ zuì	request punishment for death	4
130	驱车	*phr.*	qū chē	drive a chariot	4
131	权威性	*n.*	quán wēi xìng	authoritativeness	2
132	劝导	*v.*	quàn dǎo	guide，advise	12
133	缺一不可	*idm.*	quē yī bù kě	indispensable，essential	12
134	融入	*v.*	róng rù	integrate，merge	9
135	儒士	*n.*	rú shì	Confucianism scholar	5
136	入朝	*phr.*	rù cháo	attend court	4
137	删减	*v.*	shān jiǎn	cut down，reduce	11
138	擅兴	*proper n.*	Shàn xīng	law about act without permission	12
139	上层建筑	*n.*	shàng céng jiàn zhù	superstructure	5
140	尚德	*v.*	shàng dé	value virtue	3
141	尚书令	*n.*	shàng shū lìng	an official title in ancient Chinese government	9
142	上位者	*n.*	shàng wèi zhě	those in superior positions	4

续表

序号	生词	词性	汉语拼音	英文解释	所在课文
143	上下	*phr.*	shàng xià	senior and junior	7
144	社稷	*n.*	shè jì	national altar (sovereignty)	4
145	赦免	*v.*	shè miǎn	pardon，forgive	9
146	神判	*n.*	shén pàn	divine judgement	2
147	神权	*n.*	shén quán	theocratic authority	9
148	神圣性	*n.*	shén shèng xìng	sanctity	2
149	神农	*proper n.*	Shén nóng	name of a legendary ruler	1
150	审理	*v.*	shěn lǐ	adjudicate	10
151	慎罚	*v.*	shèn fá	administer punishment cautiously	3
152	升级	*v.*	shēng jí	upgrade	11
153	师范	*n.*	shī fàn	role model	10
154	施行	*v.*	shī xíng	implement，carry out	2
155	使命	*n.*	shǐ mìng	mission	6
156	事律	*n.*	shì lǜ	laws regarding affairs	12
157	适用范围	*phr.*	shì yòng fàn wéi	scope of application	9
158	士卒	*n.*	shì zú	soldiers，troops	8
159	守护	*v.*	shǒu hù	guard，protect	4
160	疏导	*v.*	shū dǎo	dredge，divert	1
161	赎	*v.*	shú	redeem	11
162	赎刑	*n.*	shú xíng	redemption of punishment	11
163	束矢	*n.*	shù shǐ	a bundle of arrows，metaphor for legal fee	3
164	水利工程	*n.*	shuǐ lì gōng chéng	hydraulic engineering	1
165	税收标准	*phr.*	shuì shōu biāo zhǔn	tax standards	1

续表

序号	生词	词性	汉语拼音	英文解释	所在课文
166	司寇	n.	sī kòu	minister of justice	3
167	死刑	n.	sǐ xíng	capital punishment	10
168	讼	n.	sòng	lawsuit，litigation	3
169	隋书	proper n.	Suí Shū	Book of Sui	11
170	隋文帝	proper n.	Suí wén dì	Emperor Wen of Sui	11
171	隋炀帝	proper n.	Suí yáng dì	Emperor Yang of Sui	11
172	汤誓	proper n.	Tāng shì	Oath of King Tang	2
173	替代	v.	tì dài	replace	9
174	天命神权	n.	tiān mìng shén quán	divine right of kings	3
175	条款	n.	tiáo kuǎn	clause，provision	9
176	挑战	n.	tiǎo zhàn	challenge	6
177	统帅	n.	tǒng shuài	commander-in-chief	8
178	统治地位	n.	tǒng zhì dì wèi	position of rule	5
179	统治阶层	phr.	tǒng zhì jiē céng	ruling class	2
180	推崇	v.	tuī chóng	highly respect or advocate	7
181	完备	adj.	wán bèi	complete，comprehensive	11
182	威严	n.	wēi yán	dignity，majesty	4
183	维护	v.	wéi hù	maintain，uphold	9
184	稳定	adj.	wěn dìng	stable	9
185	夏氏	proper n.	Xià shì	the Xia clan	2
186	下位者	n.	xià wèi zhě	those in inferior positions	4
187	向善	v.	xiàng shàn	turn to goodness	12
188	小宗	n.	xiǎo zōng	secondary branch of a family	3
189	绡纱	n.	xiāo shā	silk gauze	8

续表

序号	生词	词性	汉语拼音	英文解释	所在课文
190	挟书律	*proper n.*	Xié shū Lǜ	law against private possession of books	5
191	谢罪	*phr.*	xiè zuì	apologize for a crime	8
192	刑罚制度	*phr.*	xíng fá zhì dù	penal system	1
193	修订	*v.*	xiū dìng	revise	11
194	宣称	*v.*	xuān chēng	proclaim，declare	2
195	轩辕	*proper n.*	Xuān yuán	name of Yellow Emperor	1
196	巡视	*v.*	xún shì	inspect	1
197	严苛	*adj.*	yán kē	harsh，severe	6
198	严厉	*adj.*	yán lì	strict，severe	8
199	阳秋	*phr.*	yáng qiū	spring and autumn	12
200	依据	*prep.*	yī jù	according to	2
201	以古非今	*idm.*	yǐ gǔ fēi jīn	criticize the present by praising the past	5
202	劓	*n.*	yì	nose cutting punishment	3
203	佚失	*v.*	yì shī	lose	11
204	姻亲	*n.*	yīn qīn	relation by marriage	7
205	影响力	*n.*	yǐng xiǎng lì	influence	9
206	狱	*n.*	yù	prison，legal case	3
207	圜土	*n.*	yuán tǔ	prison，a type of labor punishment	3
208	越界	*v.*	yuè jiè	overstep boundaries	4
209	云师	*proper n.*	Yún shī	title of an official	1
210	杂律	*proper n.*	Zá lǜ	miscellaneous laws	12
211	诈伪	*proper n.*	Zhà wěi	fraud and deceit	12
212	斩杀	*v.*	zhǎn shā	behead，kill	4
213	长幼	*phr.*	zhǎng yòu	elders and youngsters	7

续表

序号	生词	词性	汉语拼音	英文解释	所在课文
214	杖刑	n.	zhàng xíng	punishment of beating	11
215	赵郡王	n.	Zhào jùn wáng	title of a noble in ancient China	9
216	赭衣塞路	idm.	zhě yī sè lù	people in prison garb fill the roads	5
217	贞问	n.	zhēn wèn	divination inquiry	2
218	征	v.	zhēng	conquer，campaign	1
219	征伐	v.	zhēng fá	campaign against，attack	2
220	政策改革	phr.	zhèng cè gǎi gé	policy reform	6
221	止奸	phr.	zhǐ jiān	stop treachery	12
222	旨意	n.	zhǐ yì	will，intention	2
223	制度	n.	zhì dù	system，institution	5
224	治国	phr.	zhì guó	govern a country	6
225	置喙	v.	zhì huì	meddle，interfere	2
226	治理	n.	zhì lǐ	administration	11
227	秩序	n.	zhì xù	order，sequence	9
228	重罪	n.	zhòng zuì	serious crime，felony	9
229	主簿	n.	zhǔ bù	official in charge of paperwork	8
230	专心致志	idm.	zhuān xīn zhì zhì	concentrate wholly on	10
231	装饰	n.	zhuāng shì	decoration	7
232	庄重	adj.	zhuāng zhòng	solemn，dignified	7
233	自首	phr.	zì shǒu	surrender oneself	8
234	奏请	v.	zòu qǐng	petition	10
235	宗法制	n.	zōng fǎ zhì	clan system	3
236	宗庙	n.	zōng miào	ancestral temple	4
237	族群	n.	zú qún	ethnic group，tribe	2
238	罪律	n.	zuì lǜ	criminal laws	12

续表

序号	生词	词性	汉语拼音	英文解释	所在课文
239	尊崇	*v.*	zūn chóng	revere，esteem	2
240	尊贵	*adj.*	zūn guì	noble，distinguished	8
241	尊尊	*phr.*	zūn zūn	respect the respectable	3

课前准备生词表汇总

序号	生词	词性	汉语拼音	英文解释	所在课文
1	八王之乱	*proper n.*	Bā Wáng zhī Luàn	The War of Eight Princes	8
2	罢黜百家	*phr.*	bà chù bǎi jiā	dismiss all other schools of thought	6
3	傍章律	*proper n.*	Bàng zhāng Lù	the law about etiquette	7
4	暴虐无道	*idm.*	bào nüè wú dào	tyrannical and unjust	5
5	北朝	*proper n.*	Běi Cháo	Northern Dynasties	8
6	北齐	*proper n.*	Běi Qí	Northern Qi dynasty	8
7	北周	*proper n.*	Běi Zhōu	Northern Zhou dynasty	8
8	变法	*n.*	biàn fǎ	pditical reform	4
9	剥削	*v.*	bō xuē	exploit	5
10	伯侯	*n.*	bó hóu	marquis, feudal lord	3
11	捕亡	*proper n.*	Bǔ wáng	the law on arrest of criminals	10
12	曹魏	*proper n.*	Cáo Wèi	a state in the Three Kingdoms	8
13	长足	*adj.*	cháng zú	rapid, substantial	7
14	朝贺	*n.*	cháo hè	morning greeting（to the emperor）	7
15	朝律	*proper n.*	Cháo Lù	the law about the minister congratulate the emperor	7
16	朝贺律	*proper n.*	Cháo hè Lù	another name for "Morning Court Law"	7
17	陈	*proper n.*	Chén	Chen dynasty	8
18	称雄	*v.*	chēng xióng	claim hegemony	5
19	成宪	*n.*	chéng xiàn	established legal system	7
20	丞相	*n.*	chéng xiàng	prime minister	5
21	出土	*v.*	chū tǔ	unearth, excavate	2
22	楚汉争霸	*phr.*	Chǔ Hàn zhēng bà	Chu-Han contention	6
23	传统律典	*n.*	chuán tǒng lù diǎn	traditional code of laws	10

续表

序号	生词	词性	汉语拼音	英文解释	所在课文
24	篡位	v.	cuàn wèi	usurp the throne	8
25	大一统	n.	dà yī tǒng	grand unification	6
26	代表性	n.	dài biǎo xìng	representativeness	9
27	道德	n.	dào dé	morality	9
28	德礼	n.	dé lǐ	virtue and etiquette	11
29	德治	n.	dé zhì	rule by virtue	11
30	定分止争	idm.	dìng fēn zhǐ zhēng	define roles to prevent disputes	4
31	东魏	proper n.	Dōng Wèi	Eastern Wei dynasty	8
32	豆	n.	dòu	vessel (in ancient contexts)	1
33	都护府	n.	dū hù fǔ	Protectorate	6
34	独尊儒术	phr.	dú zūn rú shù	solely honor Confucianism	6
35	断狱	proper n.	Duàn yù	the law about adjudication	10
36	法令	n.	fǎ lìng	laws and decrees	12
37	法律化	v.	fǎ lù huà	legalization	9
38	法律史	n.	fǎ lù shǐ	legal history	1
39	法治	n.	fǎ zhì	rule of law	5
40	法治思想	phr.	fǎ zhì sī xiǎng	legal philosophy	12
41	法则	n.	fǎ zé	rule, principle	3
42	繁复	adj.	fán fù	complicated, complex	12
43	繁密	adj.	fán mì	complex, intricate	7
44	烦琐	adj.	fán suǒ	cumbersome, tedious	12
45	废除	v.	fèi chú	abolish, repeal	12
46	分工	v.	fēn gōng	division of labor	10
47	分裂	n.	fēn liè	division, split	11
48	分则	n.	fēn zé	specific rules	10
49	焚书坑儒	idm.	fén shū kēng rú	burning of books and burying of Confucianism scholars	5

续表

序号	生词	词性	汉语拼音	英文解释	所在课文
50	封	v.	fēng	confer a title or land	3
51	改元	phr.	gǎi yuán	change the era name	11
52	高贵	adj.	gāo guì	noble	9
53	高祖	n.	gāo zǔ	high ancestor, title for an emperor	7
54	格式	n.	gé shì	format, style	12
55	割据	v.	gē jù	rule over separate territories	5
56	供奉	v.	gòng fèng	offer sacrifices to the gods	1
57	管仲	proper n.	Guǎn Zhòng	famous strategist	4
58	光武中兴	proper n.	Guāng wǔ Zhōng xīng	restoration of Eastern Han by Emperor Guangwu	7
59	韩非	proper n.	Hán Fēi	legalist philosopher	4
60	寒门	n.	hán mén	poor families	9
61	好耕农	phr.	hào gēng nóng	skilled in farming	3
62	后稷	proper n.	Hòu jì	mythical ancestor	3
63	皇帝	n.	huáng dì	emperor	6
64	黄巾起义	proper n.	Huáng jīn Qǐ yì	Yellow Turbans Uprising	8
65	会意字	n.	huì yì zì	ideogram	1
66	激化	v.	jī huà	intensify	11
67	祭神求福	phr.	jì shén qiú fú	worship gods and seek blessings	1
68	姬氏	proper n.	Jī shì	the Ji clan	3
69	甲骨文	n.	jiǎ gǔ wén	oracle bone script	1
70	稼穑	n.	jià sè	farming and harvesting	3
71	简约	adj.	jiǎn yuē	simple and concise	12
72	建立	v.	jiàn lì	establish, set up	2
73	建康	proper n.	Jiàn kāng	ancient city in China	8

续表

序号	生词	词性	汉语拼音	英文解释	所在课文
74	谨慎	*adj.*	jǐn shèn	cautious, prudent	12
75	精简	*v.*	jīng jiǎn	streamline	10
76	九品中正制	*proper n.*	Jiǔ pǐn Zhōng zhèng Zhì	a method of selecting officials	9
77	九章律	*proper n.*	Jiǔ zhāng Lǜ	the main body of Han Law	7
78	军阀	*n.*	jūn fá	warlord	8
79	君主专制	*n.*	jūn zhǔ zhuān zhì	autocracy, absolute monarchy	5
80	郡县制	*n.*	jùn xiàn zhì	system of prefectures and counties	5
81	宽松	*adj.*	kuān sōng	relaxed, loose	12
82	匮乏	*adj.*	kuì fá	scarce, insufficient	2
83	梁	*proper n.*	Liáng	Liang dynasty	8
84	留守	*n.*	liú shǒu	a temporary military office	11
85	刘蜀	*proper n..*	Liú Shǔ	a state in the Three Kingdoms	8
86	洛邑	*proper n.*	Luò yì	ancient city	3
87	礼崩乐坏	*idm.*	lǐ bēng yuè huài	collapse of rites and music (chaos)	4
88	礼仪	*n.*	lǐ yí	etiquette	9
89	立法	*v.*	lì fǎ	legislate	7
90	零散	*adj.*	líng sǎn	fragmented, scattered	2
91	律典	*n.*	lǜ diǎn	code of laws	10
92	律令	*n.*	lǜ lìng	system of laws and decrees	10
93	律学	*n.*	lǜ xué	jurisprudence	10
94	掠夺	*v.*	lüè duó	plunder, loot	3
95	门阀	*n.*	mén fá	influential families	9
96	灭亡	*v.*	miè wáng	perish, be annihilated	12

序号	生词	词性	汉语拼音	英文解释	所在课文
97	名例	*proper n.*	Míng lì	the law about penal names and examples	10
98	牧野	*proper n.*	Mù yě	historical site	3
99	南朝	*proper n.*	Nán Cháo	Southern Dynasties	8
100	南下	*phr.*	nán xià	move or advance southward	11
101	农民起义	*phr.*	nóng mín qǐ yì	peasant uprising	5
102	农师	*n.*	nóng shī	agricultural instructor	3
103	篇幅	*n.*	piān fú	length of a document	10
104	篇目	*n.*	piān mù	chapters and sections	10
105	贫民	*n.*	pín mín	poor people	9
106	品官占田荫客制	*proper n.*	Pǐn guān Zhàn tián Yìn kè Zhì	system of guaranteeing the economic privileges of the aristocracy and the bureaucracy	9
107	齐	*proper n.*	Qí	Qi dynasty	8
108	轻法	*n.*	qīng fǎ	lenient law	7
109	轻缓	*adj.*	qīng huǎn	lenient, mild	12
110	权臣	*n.*	quán chén	powerful official	8
111	全面	*adj.*	quán miàn	comprehensive	7
112	仁政	*n.*	rén zhèng	benevolent governance	11
113	儒家化	*n.*	rú jiā huà	Confucianization	9
114	三足鼎立	*idm.*	sān zú dǐng lì	tripartite confrontation	8
115	商汤	*proper n.*	Shāng Tāng	King Tang of Shang	2
116	商纣王	*proper n.*	Shāng zhòu wáng	King Zhou of Shang	2
117	盛世	*n.*	shèng shì	golden age, period of prosperity	11
118	实践经验	*n.*	shí jiàn jīng yàn	practical experience	12
119	实体法	*n.*	shí tǐ fǎ	substantive law	10

续表

序号	生词	词性	汉语拼音	英文解释	所在课文
120	实用	*adj.*	shí yòng	practical, pragmatic	12
121	始祖	*n.*	shǐ zǔ	ancestor	3
122	势家	*n.*	shì jiā	powerful families	9
123	士族	*n.*	shì zú	aristocratic clans	9
124	衰微	*adj.*	shuāi wēi	declined, weak	4
125	丝绸之路	*proper n.*	Sī chóu zhī lù	Silk Road	6
126	司马氏	*proper n.*	Sī mǎ shì	Sima clan	8
127	司马炎	*proper n..*	Sī mǎ Yán	Emperor Wu of Jin	8
128	宋	*proper n.*	Sòng	Liu Song dynasty	8
129	泰始律	*proper n.*	Tài shǐ Lù	laws of the Taishi era	10
130	太尉	*n.*	tài wèi	grand commandant	5
131	探索	*v.*	tàn suǒ	explore	10
132	体例	*n.*	tǐ lì	structure and style	10
133	调整	*v.*	tiáo zhěng	adjust	10
134	天下共主	*n.*	tiān xià gòng zhǔ	ruler of all under heaven	4
135	统一	*v.*	tǒng yī	unify	11
136	统治者	*n.*	tǒng zhì zhě	ruler	12
137	退位	*v.*	tuì wèi	abdicate	11
138	拓跋氏	*proper n.*	Tuò bá shì	Tuoba clan, founders of Northern Wei	8
139	外戚	*n.*	wài qī	relatives by marriage (of the ruling family)	11
140	王朝	*n.*	wáng cháo	dynasty	2
141	卫禁	*proper n.*	Wèi jìn	the law about guards and prohibitions	10

序号	生词	词性	汉语拼音	英文解释	所在课文
142	文景之世	*phr.*	wén jǐng zhī shì	the era of Emperors Wen and Jing of Han dynasty	7
143	文献	*n.*	wén xiàn	documents, archives	2
144	西魏	*proper n.*	Xī Wèi	Western Wei dynasty	8
145	夏桀	*proper n.*	Xià Jié	King Jie of Xia	2
146	夏启	*proper n.*	Xià Qǐ	King Qi of Xia	2
147	相地	*phr.*	xiàng dì	survey the land	3
148	相沿	*v.*	xiāng yán	follow, be in line with	7
149	刑罚	*n.*	xíng fá	penalties, punishments	11
150	行礼之器	*n.*	xíng lǐ zhī qì	ritual vessel	1
151	匈奴	*proper n.*	Xiōng nú	Xiongnu, an ancient nomadic tribe	6
152	休养生息	*phr.*	xiū yǎng shēng xī	recuperate and multiply	6
153	血缘	*n.*	xuè yuán	blood relation	9
154	一级字	*n.*	yī jí zì	first-level character (in complexity)	1
155	仪典	*n.*	yí diǎn	ceremony	1
156	殷	*proper n.*	Yīn	another name for Shang dynasty	2
157	引礼入法	*phr.*	yǐn lǐ rù fǎ	integrate rites into laws	1
158	影响	*n.*	yǐng xiǎng	influence	11
159	御史大夫	*n.*	yù shǐ dà fū	imperial censor	5
160	寓言	*n.*	yù yán	fable, parable	4
161	约法三章	*idm.*	yuē fǎ sān zhāng	three-point covenant	7
162	越宫律	*proper n.*	Yuè gōng Lǜ	the law about the palace guards	7
163	争鸣	*v.*	zhēng míng	contend vocally, debate	4

续表

序号	生词	词性	汉语拼音	英文解释	所在课文
164	争于气力	*idm.*	zhēng yú qì lì	struggle for power and strength	4
165	职制	*proper n.*	Zhí zhì	the law about system of official duties	10
166	中央集权	*n.*	zhōng yāng jí quán	centralization of power	5
167	重农抑商	*idm.*	zhòng nóng yì shāng	prioritize agriculture over commerce	5
168	众叛亲离	*idm.*	zhòng pàn qīn lí	everyone forsakes one	3
169	重视	*v.*	zhòng shì	value	9
170	专制主义	*n.*	zhuān zhì zhǔ yì	totalitarianism	5
171	资料	*n.*	zī liào	materials, data	2
172	子产	*proper n.*	Zǐ chǎn	statesman of Zheng	4
173	宗法	*n.*	zōng fǎ	clan law	9
174	总则	*n.*	zǒng zé	general rules	10
175	祖宗	*n.*	zǔ zōng	ancestor	7
176	尊王攘夷	*idm.*	zūn wáng rǎng yí	honor the king and repel the barbarians	4